LINCOLN
In His Own Words

Also by Milton Meltzer

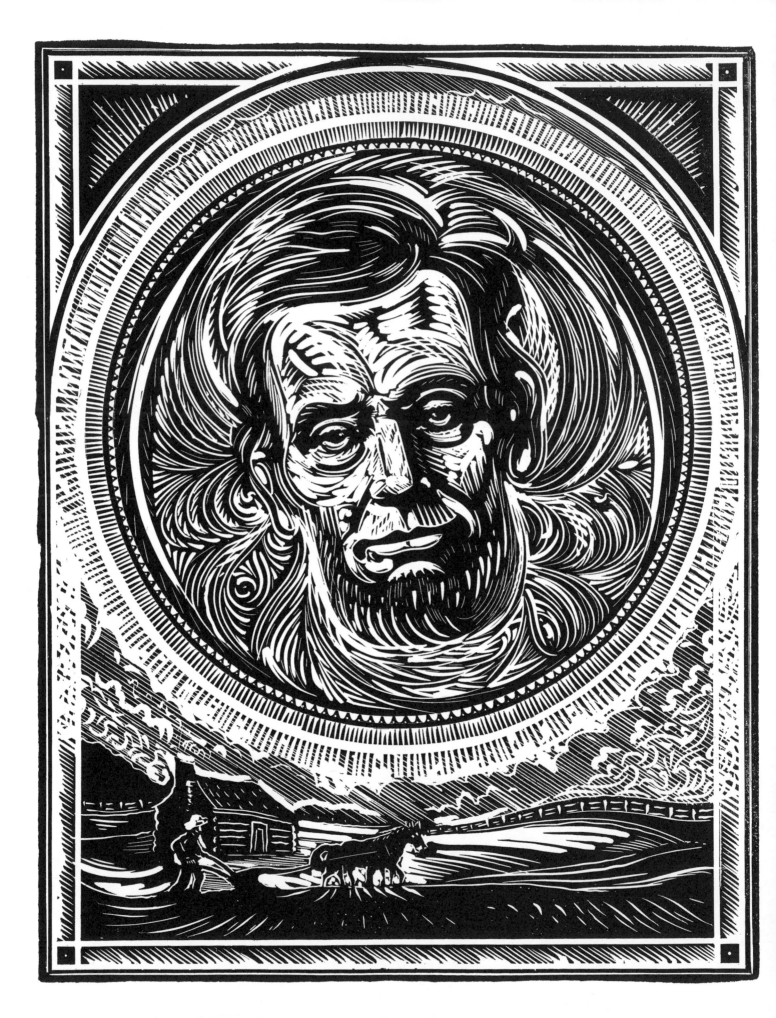

LINCOLN
In His Own Words

EDITED BY

Milton Meltzer

ILLUSTRATED BY

Stephen Alcorn

Harcourt Brace & Company
SAN DIEGO   NEW YORK   LONDON

Requests for permission to make copies of any part
of the work should be mailed to: Permissions Department,
Harcourt Brace & Company, 8th Floor,
Orlando, Florida 32887.

Library of Congress Cataloging-in-Publication Data
Lincoln: in his own words/edited by Milton Meltzer;
illustrated by Stephen Alcorn.—1st ed.
p.   cm.
Includes bibliographical references and index.
Summary: Combines background commentary with quotes
from Lincoln's letters, speeches, and public papers to
provide a personal view of his life, thoughts, and actions.
ISBN 0-15-245437-3
ISBN 0-15-245438-1 (ltd. ed.)
1. United States—Politics and government—1849–1861.
2. United States—Politics and government—Civil War, 1861–1865.
3. Lincoln, Abraham, 1809–1865—Political and social views.
[1. Lincoln, Abraham, 1809–1865.   2. Presidents.]
I. Meltzer, Milton, 1915–
II. Alcorn, Stephen, ill.
E457.92   1993
973.7'092—dc20   92-17431

Designed by Michael Farmer and John Alcorn
First edition
A B C D E

Printed in Singapore

To my wife, Hildy

—M. M.

In memory of my father,
John Alcorn
1935–1992
Visse d'arte, visse d'amore

—S.A.

Contents

Author's Note

ABRAHAM LINCOLN'S NAME IS MAGIC. MANY AMERICANS, YOUNG AND OLD, cherish an image of the man. His name is everywhere: on street and city, park and playground, school and university, museum and monument and arts center. Even business enterprise, from banking and insurance to neighborhood laundry and coffee shop, seeks shelter under the great name.

There seems to be no end to books about Lincoln. More have been written about him than anyone except Jesus and Shakespeare. Then why still another? Because most of the books give you Lincoln in the words of the biographer or historian who looks at him. Except for the Gettysburg Address, there is little or nothing of Lincoln in his own words for young readers: what he said or wrote about, what he thought, felt, and did. Yet few Americans' words are more worth knowing. For Lincoln, as is commonly agreed, was one of the greatest masters of the English language. He had a gift for writing that placed him far above his contemporaries. Most historians today believe he was not only our greatest president but the greatest writer among our presidents.

The foremost authors of Lincoln's own time, such as Ralph Waldo Emerson, Nathaniel Hawthorne, and Walt Whitman, praised Lincoln's genius with words. Words both powerful and lyrical about democracy and freedom and equality, words that still stir the mind and touch the heart.

In his years of public life, Lincoln composed more than one million words. They are found in letters, in notes on remarks he made privately and on public occasions, and, of course, in his speeches and presidential papers. The record of those words has been gathered and published in a few scholarly editions (listed in "A Note on Sources").

My aim is to share with the reader the strength and beauty, the humor and wit, the tenderness and compassion, the wisdom and insight of Lincoln's own words. While the book moves through the stages of his life, there is no attempt to fill in every corner of his story or to trace the course of the Civil War in detail. At times, when it seemed right, I have taken a number of things Lincoln said on an important subject at different periods of his life and presented them together.

Lincoln was not rigid in his thinking, but flexible. He adapted himself to changing circumstances without losing sight of fundamental principles. As executive head of government and chief of the armed forces during the Civil War—a time of crisis and rapid political and military movement— his views or tactics shifted to meet the practical necessities as he understood them. For us today his words provide many a lesson on the connection between personality and politics.

A word about the text: A brief commentary introduces each section or passage to help the reader understand what was happening at that particular moment of Lincoln's life and to suggest its historical significance. Some of the documents are given in full. In many I have taken the liberty of selecting those parts that I think will be of greater interest to readers. Anyone who wishes to read the full documents will be able to find them listed in the sources given at the back of the book. Cuts in documents are indicated by ellipses (. . .). Paragraphing, punctuation, capitalization, and spelling have been modernized for easier reading.

Readers will note that each chapter of this book opens with a portrait of an important figure from the Lincoln years. They range from Thomas Jefferson, whose ideas about equality and freedom influenced young Lincoln, to Ulysses S. Grant, whose military prowess brought the Civil War to its conclusion. Opponents and defenders of slavery are both depicted, to suggest the contending forces Lincoln had to deal with. A brief profile of each person portrayed can be found on pages 197–205.

—Milton Meltzer

1

A
PASSION
WITHIN
ME

LINCOLN NEVER SAID MUCH IN PRINT about his childhood. In 1859, when people began to talk about him as a possible candidate for president, he was asked to provide a brief autobiography for campaign use. He thought there was nothing in his early history that would interest anyone. And, he said, "I do not think myself fit for the presidency." Still, he went on, "I admit I am ambitious and would like to be president."

So he did write something, but it was only the bare facts. If he had not become president, no one would bother to read it. Now, looking back on his life, his beginnings mean so much more. He was born in a log cabin in the slave state of Kentucky on February 12, 1809. He came from a long line of pioneers who since the 1600s had been inching their way west from the Atlantic coast. He was the son of the illiterate carpenter-farmer, Thomas Lincoln, and Nancy Hanks Lincoln. His boyhood was spent in the new free state of Indiana, in a ceaseless struggle against hardship and poverty. His mother died when he was nine, and the next year his father was remarried, to the widow Sarah Johnston, who had three children of her own. Lincoln seems not to have been close to his father; why, he never explained.

Add up all the days Lincoln spent in this school or that, and they come to less than a year. The frontier teachers were expected to know little more than "readin', writin', and cipherin'," he said. If a straggler came by who claimed he knew Latin, he was looked upon as a wizard. Few books came to the boy's hand, but they were good ones. He read the family Bible, John Bunyan's *Pilgrim's Progress*, Daniel Defoe's *Robinson Crusoe*, Aesop's *Fables*, and a history of the United States. And then there was the very popular, myth-making *Life of George Washington* by Mason Locke Weems. Lincoln tells what that last book meant to him:

> **Away back in my childhood, the earliest days of my being able to read, I got hold of a small book, such a one as few of the younger members have ever seen, Weems' *Life of George Washington*. I remember all the accounts there given of the battlefields and struggles for the liberties of the country, and none fixed themselves upon my imagination so deeply as the struggle here at Trenton, New Jersey. The crossing of the river, the contest with the Hessians, the great hardships endured at that time, all fixed themselves on my memory more than any single revolutionary event; and you all know, for you have all been boys, how these early impressions last longer than any others. I recollect thinking then, boy even though I was, that there must have been something more than common that those men struggled for.**

Lincoln liked to read poetry, too. His favorite poets were Robert Burns, Lord Byron, and above all Shakespeare. He knew much of their work by heart and enjoyed reciting their lines. It helped to shape his natural talent for vivid and forceful speech. His concern for clarity and simplicity in the use of language started early. He wanted everyone to understand exactly what he meant when he spoke or wrote. Once, when asked why this mattered so much to him, he replied:

Thomas Jefferson

Among my earliest recollections I remember how, when a mere child, I used to get irritated when anybody talked to me in a way I could not understand. . . . I can remember going to my little bedroom, after hearing the neighbors talk of an evening with my father, and spending the night walking up and down and trying to make out what was the exact meaning of some of their, to me, dark sayings. I could not sleep . . . when I got on such a hunt after an idea, until I had caught it; and when I thought I had got it, I was not satisfied . . . until I had put it in language plain enough, as I thought, for any boy I knew to comprehend. This was a kind of passion with me, and it has stuck by me.

In his teens Lincoln did many odd jobs, seasonal mostly, to earn his keep. At nineteen, he and another young man stowed farm produce on a flatboat and took it down the Ohio and the Mississippi to sell in New Orleans. There, in the slave market, he saw black men, women, and children auctioned off to the highest bidders. Later, while traveling down the Ohio on a steamboat, he observed another aspect of slavery that would be "a continual torment" to him. He described the scene in a letter to a Kentucky friend, Mary Speed:

A fine example was presented on board the boat for contemplating the effect of condition upon human happiness. A gentleman had purchased twelve Negroes in different parts of Kentucky and was taking them to a farm in the South. They were chained six and six together. A small iron clevis was around the left wrist of each, and this fastened to the main chain by a shorter one at a convenient distance from the others, so that the Negroes were strung together precisely like so many fish upon a trotline. In this condition they were being separated forever from the scenes of their childhood, their friends, their fathers and mothers, and brothers and sisters, and many of them, from their wives and children, and going into perpetual slavery, where the lash of the master is proverbially more ruthless and unrelenting than any otherwhere; and yet amid all these distressing circumstances, as we would think them, they were the most cheerful and apparently happy creatures on board. One, whose offense for which he had been sold was an over-fondness for his wife, played the fiddle almost continually; and the others danced, sang, cracked jokes, and played various games with cards from day to day. How true it is that "God tempers the wind to the shorn lamb," or in other words, that He renders the worst of human conditions tolerable, while He permits the best to be nothing better than tolerable.

Turning twenty, Lincoln began to hang around county courthouses. He was drawn by the drama of trials, the clash of lawyers, the passionate appeals to juries, the rulings of judges. Determined to understand the roots of the system of justice, he began studying the Declaration of Independence and the Constitution and reading law books.

What he learned about the American Revolution made him see both its glory and its cost:

If the relative grandeur of revolutions shall be estimated by the great amount of human misery they alleviate and the small amount they inflict, then, indeed, will this be the grandest the world shall ever have seen. Of our political revolution of '76 we all are justly proud. It has given us a degree of political freedom far exceeding that of any other of the nations of the earth. In it the world has found a solution of the long mooted problem as to the capability of

7

man to govern himself. In it was the germ which was vege-
tated and still is to grow and expand into the universal
liberty of mankind.

But with all these glorious results—past, present, and to
come—it had its evils, too. It breathed forth famine, swam
in blood, and rode on fire; and long, long after, the orphan's
cry and the widow's wail continued to break the sad silence
that ensued. These were the price, the inevitable price, paid
for the blessings it bought.

At twenty-two, Lincoln left home and settled in New Salem, a pioneer
village of Illinois, where he took a job as clerk in the general store. A
few older and well-educated men befriended the newcomer and encouraged
his hunger for knowledge. He joined the local debating club, studied
oratory, made his first speeches, learned basic mathematics, and practiced
his writing.

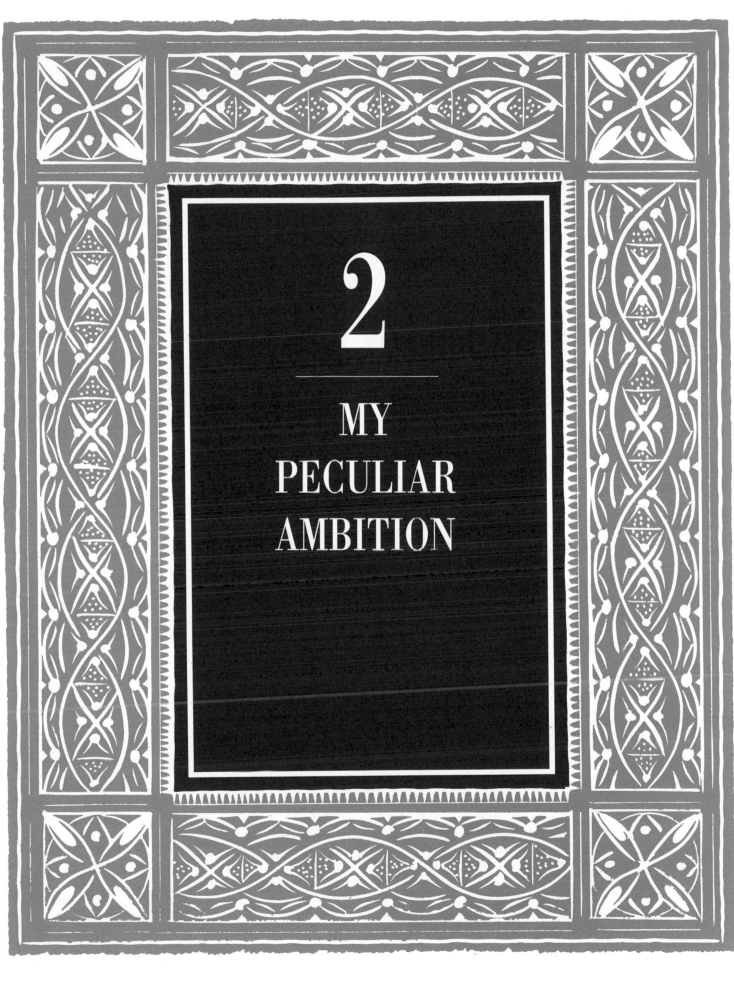

2

MY
PECULIAR
AMBITION

I N NEW SALEM, LINCOLN'S APPE-
tite for politics began to grow. He became a follower of Henry Clay, the
national leader of the new Whig Party, rival to the older Democratic Party
led by Andrew Jackson. Both parties appealed to the mass of ordinary
Americans and advocated equal opportunity for all. The Democrats believed that the federal government should be weak and the states strong.
The Whigs, in contrast, wanted to build up America's national strength
by developing the economy and encouraging manufacturing and banking.
Clay hoped slavery would gradually be done away with and the blacks
shipped back to Africa. The Southern Democrats, who dominated the
Congress, supported slavery and resisted any attempt to restrict its spread
to new territory.

Sticking to local issues, Lincoln studied ways to improve river trans-
portation so as to make New Salem a lively commercial center. His energy,
his humor, his honesty, and his great intelligence made him a popular
figure in the county. At the age of twenty-three he decided to make his
first try for public office. In a leaflet he told the voters in his district what
he would do if elected to the state legislature. Coming from an uneducated
family, he knew how important schooling was:

Upon the subject of education, not presuming to dictate
any plan or system respecting it, I can only say that I view

it as the most important subject which we as a people can be engaged in. That every man may receive at least a moderate education, and thereby be enabled to read the histories of his own and other countries, by which he may duly appreciate the value of our free institutions, appears to be an object of vital importance, even on this account alone, to say nothing of the advantages and satisfaction to be derived from all being able to read the Scriptures and other works, both of a religious and moral nature, for themselves. For my part, I desire to see the time when education, and by its means, morality, sobriety, enterprise, and industry, shall become much more general than at present, and should be gratified to have it in my power to contribute something to the advancement of any measure which might have a tendency to accelerate the happy period.

In the same message to voters, he spoke of both modesty and ambition:

Considering the great degree of modesty which should always attend youth, it is probable I have already been more presuming than becomes me. However, upon the subjects of which I have treated, I have spoken as I thought. I may be wrong in regard to any or all of them; but holding it a sound maxim that it is better to be only sometimes right, than at all times wrong, so soon as I discover my opinions to be erroneous, I shall be ready to renounce them.

Every man is said to have his peculiar ambition. Whether it be true or not, I can say for one that I have no other so great as that of being truly esteemed of my fellow men, by rendering myself worthy of their esteem. How far I shall succeed in gratifying this ambition is yet to be de-

William Lloyd Garrison

veloped. I am young and unknown to many of you. I was born and have ever remained in the most humble walks of life. I have no wealthy or popular relations to recommend me. My case is thrown exclusively upon the independent voters of this county, and if elected they will have conferred a favor upon me, for which I shall be unremitting in my labors to compensate. But if the good people in their wisdom shall see fit to keep me in the background, I have been too familiar with disappointments to be very much chagrined.

He lost that election. But Lincoln didn't stop dreaming about political honors. And he took practical steps to satisfy his ambition. What they were he revealed in this letter of advice to his young law partner, Billy Herndon. The "Old Zach" he refers to was General Zachary Taylor, hero of the Mexican War; "Old Rough and Ready" was the Whig candidate for president in 1848:

Now as to the young men. You must not wait to be brought forward by the older men. For instance, do you suppose that I should ever have gotten into notice if I had waited to be hunted up and pushed forward by older men? You young men get together and form a Rough and Ready club, and have regular meetings and speeches. Take in everybody that you can get . . . gather up all the shrewd wild boys about town, whether just of age or little under age . . . hundreds such. Let every one play the part he can play best—some speak, some sing. . . . Your meetings will be of evenings; the older men and the women will go to hear you. It will not only contribute to the election of "Old Zach" but will be an interesting pastime and improving to the intellectual faculties of all engaged. Don't fail to do this.

In 1832, the same year Lincoln ran for the legislature and lost, he volunteered for the Illinois militia at the outbreak of the Black Hawk War. President Jackson had begun his policy of removing Native Americans from their homelands to make way for white settlers. When the Sauk and Fox Indians who were farming in Illinois were ordered to move west of the Mississippi, some, led by Chief Black Hawk, refused to obey.

It was this brief struggle that Lincoln joined. He was looking for excitement and glory, and a soldier's pay would be helpful, too. His company wandered through woods and swamps for weeks but never got close to combat before their enlistment was up. (The Native Americans were defeated.) Later, in a speech, he ridiculed himself as he made fun of political candidates who posed as military heroes. One of these braggarts was General Lewis Cass, who broke his sword rather than surrender it to the British in the War of 1812. Here Lincoln is pretending that he, too, is a military hero:

> Did you know I am a military hero? Yes sir, in the days of the Black Hawk War, I fought, bled, and came away. Speaking of General Cass's career, reminds me of my own. . . . It is quite certain I did not break my sword, for I had none to break; but I bent a musket pretty badly on one occasion. If Cass broke his sword, the idea is, he broke it in desperation; I bent the musket by accident. If General Cass went in advance of me picking huckleberries, I guess I surpassed him in charges upon the wild onions. If he saw any live, fighting Indians, it was more than I did; but I had a good many bloody struggles with the mosquitoes; and, although I never fainted from the loss of blood, I can truly say I was often very hungry. Mr. Speaker, if I should ever conclude to doff whatever our Democratic friends may suppose there is of black cockade federalism about me, and

thereupon they shall take me up as their candidate for the presidency, I protest they shall not make fun of me, as they have of General Cass, by attempting to write me into a military hero.

Back from the Black Hawk War, Lincoln ran into bad luck when his general store failed and plunged him into debt. He hired himself out at odd jobs, living as cheaply as possible to repay what he owed. Using a book of legal forms, he drew up deeds and mortgages for his neighbors. Then came his first political appointment—President Andrew Jackson made him postmaster of New Salem. The pay was small, but at least he could add to his education by reading all the newspapers the mails brought in. When new settlers began to pour into the region, the county surveyor was overwhelmed and made Lincoln his assistant. He quickly mastered a few books on the trade and helped lay out roads and the bounds for schools and towns. Still the postmaster, he would stuff letters into his hat and deliver them to the farmers on his surveying rounds.

In 1834 he made his second campaign for the state legislature, this time winning easily. Like most legislatures, this one was full of lawyers. Lincoln borrowed law books from them and studied for the bar exam. His service on a dozen committees taught him how to draft bills and resolutions and won him many influential friends. In 1836, at the age of twenty-seven, he got his license to practice law.

3

A ROVING LAWYER

As a lawyer, Lincoln would demonstrate an impressive ability to get to the heart of an issue, to analyze the arguments of his opponents and take advantage of their weaknesses, and to win juries to his side. This power of persuasion worked superbly for him in political debate as well. After many years of experience in law, he wrote down these notes of advice for would-be lawyers:

> I am not an accomplished lawyer. I find quite as much material for a lecture in those points wherein I have failed as in those wherein I have been moderately successful. The leading rule for the lawyer, as for the man of every other calling, is diligence. Leave nothing for tomorrow which can be done today. Never let your correspondence fall behind. Whatever piece of business you have in hand, before stopping, do all the labor pertaining to it which can then be done. . . .
>
> Extemporaneous speaking should be practiced and cultivated. It is the lawyer's avenue to the public. However able and faithful he may be in other respects, people are slow to bring him business if he cannot make a speech. And yet there is not a more fatal error to young lawyers than

relying too much on speech-making. If anyone, upon his rare powers of speaking, shall claim exemption from the drudgery of the law, his case is a failure in advance.

Discourage litigation. Persuade your neighbors to compromise whenever you can. Point out to them how the nominal winner is often a real loser—in fees and expenses and waste of time. As a peacemaker, the lawyer has a superior opportunity of being a good man. There will still be business enough.

Never stir up litigation. A worse man can scarcely be found than one who does this. Who can be more nearly a fiend than he who habitually overhauls the Register of Deeds in search of defects in titles, whereon to stir up strife and put money in his pocket? A moral tone ought to be infused into the profession, which should drive such men out of it.

The matter of fees is important far beyond the mere question of bread and butter involved. Properly attended to, fuller justice is done to both lawyer and client. An exorbitant fee should never be claimed. As a general rule, never take your whole fee in advance, nor any more than a small retainer. When fully paid beforehand, you are more than a common mortal if you can feel the same interest in the case as if something was still in prospect for you, as well as for your client. And when you lack interest in the case, the job will very likely lack skill and diligence in the performance. . . .

There is a vague popular belief that lawyers are necessarily dishonest. I say vague because when we consider to what extent confidence and honors are reposed in and conferred upon lawyers by the people, it appears improbable that their impression of dishonesty is very distinct and

Lydia Maria Child

vivid. Yet the impression is common—almost universal. Let no young man, choosing the law for a calling, for a moment yield to this popular belief. Resolve to be honest at all events; and if, in your own judgment, you cannot be an honest lawyer, resolve to be honest without being a lawyer. Choose some other occupation, rather than one in the choosing of which you do, in advance, consent to be a knave.

An example of Lincoln's honesty is the note he sent a client for whom he had drawn up a lease for a hotel:

Dear Sir:

I have just received yours of 16th, with check on Flagg & Savage for twenty-five dollars. You must think I am a high-priced man. You are too liberal with your money. Fifteen dollars is enough for the job. I send you a receipt for fifteen dollars and return to you a ten-dollar bill.

A year after admission to the bar, Lincoln moved to Springfield, the new state capital of Illinois. He became partner to a more experienced lawyer and soon his practice covered a wide range of civil and criminal cases. By now Lincoln was one of the leading lawmakers. He put his native tact and good humor to great use in creating compromises that advanced his political goals. Everyone recognized how shrewd he was in operating the political machinery.

In the 1830s a great movement against slavery took hold in the Northeast. Gradually it moved west as the missionaries of abolition began to form antislavery societies in Lincoln's region. Their courage was severely tested everywhere. Mobs broke up their meetings, wrecked their presses, assaulted their speakers. Merchants and manufacturers, banks and insurance companies, bishops and editors—the leaders of the community—did their best to block the abolitionists from their goals.

In Illinois the legislature passed a resolution disapproving the formation of abolitionist societies and the doctrines they promoted. While Lincoln detested slavery, he was influenced by the prejudices of the slave state he was born in and by a racism that infected people of the free states as well. Still, he drafted a resolution opposing the one just passed. It said, "The undersigned . . . believe that the institution of slavery is founded on both injustice and bad policy," but added that the agitation of the abolitionists tended "to increase rather than abate its evils." Only one other legislator was willing to join Lincoln in signing the statement, cautious as it was.

Mob violence soon erupted in Illinois. When the Reverend Elijah P. Lovejoy, editor of a St. Louis newspaper, protested the lynching of a black man, he was forced to leave town. He took his printing press up the Mississippi to Alton, Illinois, but it was seized on arrival and thrown in the river. A second and third press met the same fate, but the stubborn editor bought a fourth press and kept on publishing. A mass meeting advised him to get out of Alton. "Is this not a free state?" he replied. "Have I not the right to claim the protection of the laws? Before God and you all, I here pledge myself to continue, if need be, till death." Men fired five bullets into him, and he died, defending his press.

The Alton tragedy fused abolitionism and freedom of speech into a common cause. Soon after Lovejoy's murder, Lincoln gave a speech in January 1838 to the Young Men's Lyceum in Springfield. It was a passionate outcry against mob violence:

> I hope I am overwary, but if I am not, there is, even now, something of ill-omen amongst us. I mean the increasing disregard for law which pervades the country, the growing disposition to substitute the wild and furious passions in lieu of the sober judgment of courts, and the worse than savage mobs for the executive ministers of justice. This disposition is awfully fearful in any community; and that

it now exists in ours, though grating to our feelings to admit, it would be a violation of truth and an insult to our intelligence to deny. Accounts of outrages committed by mobs form the everyday news of the times. They have pervaded the country, from New England to Louisiana. . . .

They are not the creature of climate—neither are they confined to the slaveholding or the nonslaveholding states. Alike, they spring up among the pleasure-hunting masters of Southern slaves and the order-loving citizens of the land of steady habits. Whatever, then, their cause may be, it is common to the whole country.

It would be tedious, as well as useless, to recount the horrors of all of them. Those happening in the state of Mississippi and at St. Louis are, perhaps, the most dangerous in example and revolting to humanity. In the Mississippi case, they first commenced by hanging the regular gamblers: a set of men, certainly not following for a livelihood a very useful or very honest occupation, but one which, so far from being forbidden by the laws, was actually licensed by an act of the Legislature, passed but a single year before. Next, Negroes suspected of conspiring to raise an insurrection were caught up and hanged in all parts of the state; then, white men, supposed to be leagued with the Negroes; and finally, strangers from the neighboring states going thither on business were, in many instances, subjected to the same fate. Thus went on this process of hanging, from gamblers to Negroes, from Negroes to white citizens, and from these to strangers; till dead men were seen literally dangling from the boughs of trees upon every roadside. . . .

Turn, then, to that horror-striking scene at St. Louis. A single victim was only sacrificed there. His story is very

short and is, perhaps, the most highly tragic of anything of its length that has ever been witnessed in real life. A mulatto man, by the name of McIntosh, was seized in the street, dragged to the suburbs of the city, chained to a tree, and actually burned to death; and all within a single hour from the time he had been a freeman, attending to his own business and at peace with the world.

Such are the effects of mob law. . . . The question recurs, "How shall we fortify against it?" The answer is simple. Let every well-wisher to his posterity swear by the blood of the Revolution never to violate in the least particular the laws of our country and never to tolerate their violation by others. . . .

There is no grievance that is a fit subject of redress by mob law. In any case that arises, as for instance, the promulgation of abolitionism, one of two positions is necessarily true: that is, the thing is right within itself, and therefore deserves the protection of all law and all good citizens; or, it is wrong, and therefore proper to be prohibited by legal enactments; and in neither case is the interposition of mob law either necessary, justifiable, or excusable. . . .

As Illinois grew, new counties were formed and more courts opened up. Lincoln would leave Springfield twice a year for long travels on the circuit, driving his horse-drawn rig across the desolate prairie to defend his clients in makeshift courtrooms. The travel was hard and lonely, but he seemed to like it. He built a great reputation—"the lawyer's lawyer"—winning most of some 250 cases brought before his state's Supreme Court. The roving practice enlarged his political network of personal friends and professional colleagues.

In his late twenties, Lincoln was still a bachelor. His halfhearted

courtship of a woman visiting his town had come to nothing. Then in 1839 he met Mary Todd, daughter of a wealthy Kentucky slaveholding family and ten years younger than himself. Short, plump, flirtatious, talkative, she was drawn to the tall lawyer whose powerful urge to succeed she sensed beneath his shyness. Three years later, after a bumpy off-and-on courtship, they married. Soon after, in a letter to a friend, Lincoln remarked, "Nothing new here, except my marrying, which to me is a matter of profound wonder."

4

A
REVOLUTIONARY
RIGHT

THE LINCOLNS BEGAN THEIR MAR-
riage by moving into the Globe Tavern, paying $4.00 a week for room and
board. Deciding it was time to move up politically, Lincoln tried to get
the Whig nomination for Congress. (In his district, that meant sure
election.) But seeing he might lose out to another man, he made a deal
to avoid a party fight. In return for stepping aside this time, next time, in
1846, Lincoln would get the nomination.

While the Whigs won in Illinois, nationally the Democrats did better;
they put their man, the Tennessean James K. Polk, into the White House.
Just before Polk took office early in 1845, Texas was annexed by the
United States, a move many Northerners opposed. They feared the vast
Texas plains would be carved up into several slave states, adding still
more political power to the South. President Polk ordered General Zachary
Taylor to move his army south of the Texas border into Mexico. When the
outraged Mexicans fired in self-defense, Polk declared that a state of war
existed. His Democratic majority allowed the Congress only two hours to
debate a war bill, stampeding the Congress into hasty action.

Lincoln had set up his own law practice in 1844, taking young William
H. Herndon as partner. Herndon, an antislavery activist, probably had
some influence on Lincoln's thinking on this issue. Soon, the Lincolns'
two sons Robert and Edward were born, and Lincoln bought a house at

Eighth and Jackson streets in Springfield. (It would be their home until they moved into the White House in 1861.)

The war was all but over by the time Lincoln was elected to Congress in 1846. He won by a large majority but had over a year to wait before the Thirtieth Congress opened in December 1847. Meanwhile, he practiced law in Springfield and watched as the American forces won victories in Mexico.

The Whigs gathered evidence on how the war had begun and blamed President Polk for deceiving the nation and starting an unnecessary, unconstitutional, and unjust war. Many called the war a Southern plot to grab new lands for the expansion of slavery.

Lincoln joined the protest movement and as soon as he took his seat in the House, offered resolutions defying the president to name the spot where American blood had been shed upon American soil.

When Polk ducked the challenge, Lincoln made a fiery speech in Congress attacking the president. The speech upset Herndon, his junior law partner, who feared it would kill Lincoln's political career. In a letter to Herndon, Lincoln explained why he had to do what he did:

Your letter of the 29th January was received last night. Being exclusively a constitutional argument, I wish to submit some reflections upon it in the same spirit of kindness that I know actuates you. Let me first state what I understand to be your position. It is, that if it shall become necessary to repel invasion, the president may, without violation of the Constitution, cross the line and invade the territory of another country; and that whether such necessity exists in any given case, the president is to be the sole judge.

Before going further, consider well whether this is or is not your position. If it is, it is a position that neither the

Henry David Thoreau

president himself, nor any friend of his, so far as I know, has ever taken. Their only positions are first, that the soil was ours where hostilities commenced, and second, that whether it was rightfully ours or not, Congress had annexed it, and the president for that reason was bound to defend it, both of which are as clearly proved to be false in fact, as you can prove that your house is not mine. That soil was not ours; and Congress did not annex or attempt to annex it. But to return to your position: allow the president to invade a neighboring nation whenever he shall deem it necessary to repel an invasion, and you allow him to do so whenever he may choose to say he deems it necessary for such purpose—and you allow him to make war at pleasure.

Study to see if you can fix any limit to his power in this respect, after you have given him so much as you propose. If, today, he should choose to say he thinks it necessary to invade Canada to prevent the British from invading us, how could you stop him? You may say to him, "I see no probability of the British invading us," but he will say to you, "Be silent; I see it, if you don't."

The provision of the Constitution giving the war-making power to Congress was dictated, as I understand it, by the following reasons. Kings had always been involving and impoverishing their people in wars, pretending generally, if not always, that the good of the people was the object. This, our Convention understood to be the most oppressive of all kingly oppressions; and they resolved to so frame the Constitution that no one man should hold the power of bringing this oppression upon us. But your view destroys the whole matter and places our president where kings have always stood.

During the debate on the Mexican War, Lincoln used humor to puncture the pretense of people who denied it was a war of aggression. It reminded him, he said, of the Illinois farmer who declared, "I ain't greedy 'bout land. I only want what joins mine."

If slavery expanded, Lincoln knew it meant that all the important economic and political decisions would be made by the slave power, which would control Congress and the presidency. To prevent that, the Wilmot Proviso was introduced; it would forbid slavery in any territory annexed by the United States as a result of the Mexican War. It passed the House, with Lincoln supporting it.

But Southerners knew that if Congress ever adopted Wilmot, the spread of slavery would be checked and the political power of the slave states ended. They denied Congress's right to interfere with slavery in the territories. They argued that the territories were the common possession of all Americans. The constitutional duty of Congress was to protect slave property in the territories. Only a territory itself, when it achieved statehood, could forbid slavery, the Southerners insisted. The Wilmot Proviso was lost when the Senate voted it down.

Lincoln's family had come to Washington to live with him in a boardinghouse. But finding the capital hot and dismal, Mary took the children to Kentucky to stay with her folks. Husband and wife exchanged chatty letters often. Lincoln's indicate his affectionate concern:

> I went yesterday to hunt the little plaid stockings as you wished, but found that McKnight has quit business and Allen had not a single pair of the description you gave and only one plaid pair of any sort that I thought would fit "Eddy's dear little feet." I have a notion to make another trial tomorrow morning. . . . I wish you would enjoy yourself in every possible way. . . . Very soon after you went away, I got what I think is a very pretty set of shirt bosom

studs—modest little ones set in gold only costing 50 cents a piece or $1.50 for the whole. . . .

And you are entirely free from headache? That is good—considering it is the first spring you have been free from it since we were acquainted. I am afraid you will get so well and fat and young as to be wanting to marry again. Tell Louisa I want her to watch you a little for me. Get weighed and write me how much you weigh. . . . Don't let the blessed fellows [Robert and Edward] forget Father.

In March of 1848—only a few months after Lincoln began his one term in Congress—a peace treaty with Mexico was signed. By its terms, the United States acquired 850,000 square miles—about one-third of Mexico's land. It was larger than the combined area of France, Spain, and Italy. The nation had grown enormously by its aggression.

The war, however, did not settle the sectional conflict that would break apart both major parties. Did Congress have the right to bar slavery in the new territories? Or would they be open to free labor alone? The issue haunted the 1848 election campaign that began right after the signing of the peace treaty. Seeing how popular General Taylor's victories had made him, Lincoln's party—the Whigs—chose Taylor to be their candidate. This, even though he had shown no interest in politics, had never even bothered to vote, and owned many slaves. The antislavery Whigs didn't like this scrapping of principle. But to the politicians what counted most was winning.

By agreement with his party, Lincoln would not run for a second term in Congress, giving way to the nomination of another Whig for that office. But as a loyal party man he campaigned hard for Taylor. He took some comfort in the notion that the general would at least be a better president than anyone else who might win if Taylor didn't run. And the general did win, though just barely. What made the election close was the entry of a new party, the Free Soilers. It combined rebellious Whigs and Democrats who refused to make concessions to the South and demanded that slavery be kept out of the territories.

That year—1848—was a year of national revolutions in Europe and South America. In country after country, people rose up in arms to overthrow tyrannical regimes. In the United States, itself created by revolution, people watched hopefully. Lincoln was one of those who made public his sympathy for the oppressed. In a speech in Congress he said:

> Any people anywhere, being inclined and having the power, have the right to rise up and shake off the existing government and form a new one that suits them better. This is a most valuable, a most sacred, right—a right which we hope and believe is to liberate the world. Nor is this right confined to cases in which the whole people of an existing government may choose to exercise it. Any portion of such people that can, may revolutionize and make their own of so much of the territory as they inhabit. More than this, a majority of any portion of such people may revolutionize, putting down a minority, intermingled with or near about them, who may oppose their movement. Such minority was precisely the case of the Tories of our own revolution. It is a quality of revolutions not to go by old lines, or old law, but to break up both, and make new ones.

Later, when the Hungarian freedom fighter Lajos Kossuth visited America, a speech by Lincoln won the support of a Springfield meeting for his stand on revolution:

> It is the right of any people, sufficiently numerous for national independence, to throw off, to revolutionize their

43

existing form of government, and to establish such other in its stead as they may choose.

It is the duty of our government to neither foment nor assist such revolutions in other governments.

As we may not legally or warrantably interfere abroad, to aid, so no other government may interfere abroad, to suppress such revolutions; and that we should at once announce to the world our determination to insist upon this mutuality of nonintervention, as a sacred principle of the international law. . . .

The sympathies of this country, and the benefits of its position, should be exerted in favor of the people of every nation struggling to be free.

And finally, on the occasion of his First Inaugural Address, in 1861, Lincoln voiced the great words which, a hundred years later, were set to music and sung by artists like Paul Robeson:

This country, with its institutions, belongs to the people who inhabit it. This country, with its Constitution, belongs to those who live in it. Whenever they shall grow weary of the existing government, they can exercise their revolutionary right to dismember or overthrow it.

Like many candidates for public office, Lincoln's history was examined closely by opponents seeking to discredit him. One charge against him, raised more than once, was that he was an atheist or infidel. To counter the charge, Lincoln wrote this handbill for distribution in his congressional district:

Fellow Citizens:

A charge having got into circulation in some of the

neighborhoods of this district, in substance that I am an open scoffer at Christianity, I have by the advice of some friends concluded to notice the subject in this form. That I am not a member of any Christian church is true; but I have never denied the truth of the Scriptures; and I have never spoken with intentional disrespect of religion in general or of any denomination of Christians in particular. It is true that in early life I was inclined to believe in what I understand is called the "Doctrine of Necessity"—that is, that the human mind is impelled to action or held in rest by some power over which the mind itself has no control; and I have sometimes (with one, two, or three, but never publicly) tried to maintain this opinion in argument. The habit of arguing thus, however, I have entirely left off for more than five years. And I add here, I have always understood this same opinion to be held by several of the Christian denominations. The foregoing is the whole truth, briefly stated in relation to myself, upon this subject.

I do not think I could myself be brought to support a man for office whom I knew to be an open enemy of, and scoffer at, religion. Leaving the higher matter of eternal consequences between him and his Maker, I still do not think any man has the right thus to insult the feelings and injure the morals of the community in which he may live. If, then, I was guilty of such conduct, I should blame no man who should condemn me for it; but I do blame those, whoever they may be, who falsely put such a charge in circulation against me.

Such "negative campaigning," as we call it now, angered Lincoln. To a newspaper editor who printed the lie without checking, he said there was "one lesson in morals" that the slanderer might learn:

And that is never to add the weight of his character to a charge against his fellow man, without knowing it to be true. I believe it is an established maxim in morals that he who makes an assertion without knowing whether it is true or false, is guilty of falsehood; and the accidental truth of the assertion does not justify or excuse him. This maxim ought to be particularly held in view when we contemplate an attack upon the reputation of our neighbor.

With the 1848 election over, Lincoln returned to Congress for the last part of his sole term. The debate over slavery in the new territories heated up. Slavery became entangled with every public question of the day. Lincoln wavered for a time over how best to handle the issue. Finally he introduced a bill to abolish slavery in the District of Columbia. He felt at least this much could be done without violating the Constitution.

His bill proposed gradual emancipation of the District's slaves, with their owners to be compensated. But it also provided that fugitive slaves coming into the District must be sent back to their masters. So his proposal infuriated both the abolitionists and the Southerners. When stormy threats of secession rose from the slaveholders, Lincoln gave up on his bill. The Congress was so evenly split that no measure either for or against slavery could be adopted.

Now that he was out of Congress, what to do next? He tried but failed to get a federal appointment as land commissioner. And when offered instead the governorship of the Oregon Territory, he turned it down. It was lucky that he did, for he might have spent the rest of his days in dismal bureaucratic jobs.

Instead he went back to Springfield and the law office.

5

I LAUGH BECAUSE I MUST NOT CRY

When Lincoln and his family came home to Springfield, he picked up his law practice and put politics aside—for the moment. Early in 1850 the Lincolns lost their younger son, Eddie. Not quite four, he died after a brief illness. "We miss him very much," Lincoln wrote to his stepbrother. Mary collapsed and wept for weeks. She turned to her church for comfort, while Lincoln, trying to break out of a severe depression, plunged into his work. What helped them both was the birth, at the end of the year, of another son, Willie. Less than a week later, Lincoln's father, Thomas, died. Never close to the man, Lincoln did not travel to the funeral.

For the next several years Lincoln would be away from home half the year, broken up into two twelve-week cycles. His judicial circuit covered much of central and eastern Illinois. Since fees were low, he took all the cases he could get. Most were routine civil suits, dull to handle, but he did some more exciting criminal work, too. Henry C. Whitney, a lawyer who practiced on the circuit with him, said that "Lincoln had three different moods: first, a business mood, when he gave strict and close attention to business and banished all idea of hilarity, i.e., in counseling or in trying cases, there was no trace of the joker; second, his melancholy moods, when his whole nature was immersed in Cimmerian darkness; third, his don't-care-whether-school-keeps-or-not mood, when no irresponsible 'small boy' could be so apparently careless or reckless of consequences."

Another friend, Isaac N. Arnold, wrote that anyone entering a courtroom would instantly recognize Lincoln as "a very tall specimen of the type of long, large-boned man produced in the mountains. . . . In manner he was cordial, frank, and friendly, and although not without dignity, he put everyone perfectly at ease. The first impression a stranger meeting him or hearing him speak would receive was that of a kind, sincere, and genuinely good man of perfect truthfulness and integrity. He was one of those men whom everybody liked at first sight. If he spoke, before many words were uttered, the hearer would be impressed with his clear, direct good sense, his simple, homely, short Anglo-Saxon words, by his wonderful wit and humor."

In the courtroom give-and-take, said Whitney, Lincoln "always had a reply, and it was always pertinent, and frequently irresistibly funny, but the pity is that his funniest stories don't circulate in polite society or get embalmed in type."

Lincoln's brand of humor is acutely analyzed by Constance Rourke in her classic study, *American Humor:*

> As a storyteller Lincoln used the entire native strain; he was consistently the actor, the mimic, the caricaturist, and even a maker of burlesque. He used stories as weapons, matching his gifts against those of his adversaries, to mow them down, to win an audience. In a political contest in 1840 he mimicked his opponent on the platform in gesture and voice and walk and the smallest idiosyncrasies of manner with so bitter a ridicule that at the end the man was reduced to tears. At the bar he used the same tactics. . . .
>
> In Lincoln two of the larger strains of American comedy seemed to meet. He showed the Western ebullience, even in brief fragments. He was likely to call a bowie knife a scythe. He told of a fight in which a man fought himself out of one coat and into another. But his economy

Harriet Beecher Stowe

of speech and his laconic turn seemed derived from the Yankee strain that belonged to his ancestry, and no doubt was strengthened by many encounters with Yankees in the West. . . .

No doubt the Bible had a deep influence upon Lincoln's style in speech and in writing; perhaps it was from the Bible that he drew his deep-seated sense of fable and figure. . . . Poetry belonged to most of Lincoln's stories—an early poetry; he used the fable, the allegory, the tale grounded in metaphor. The artist was often at work there.

Some people thought it in poor taste and undignified for Lincoln to tell his stories, especially the earthier ones. But Chauncey Depew, a Republican lawyer who knew him, said that "for the person he wished to reach, and the object he desired to accomplish with the individual, the story did more than argument could have done. He once said to me in reference to some sharp criticism which had been made upon his story-telling: 'I have found in the course of a long experience that common people'—and repeating it—'common people, take them as they run, are more easily influenced and informed through the medium of a broad illustration than in any other way, and as to what the hypercritical may think, I don't care.' "

Humor, Lincoln once said, is a salve that "saves me much friction and distress." During the worst days of the Civil War he told a friend, "I laugh because I must not cry. That is all—that is all."

He liked playing upon words and was not above punning. Looking out the window of his law office one day, he watched a stately woman wearing a thickly feathered hat nervously picking her way across the muddy street, when she suddenly slipped and fell. "Reminds me of a duck," said Lincoln. "Why is that?" asked a friend. "Feathers on her head and down on her behind."

His low puns included one about Admiral Andrew Foote, whom he put in command of a naval squadron during the Civil War. Lincoln said he was sure the admiral's ship was very seaworthy. "How can you be sure?" someone asked. "Well," laughed Lincoln, "haven't I put my Foote in it?"

His humor could be sharp as a razor. Once, asked how big the Confederate Army was, he replied, "About 1,200,000 men." "What!" said his questioner, unable to believe it. Lincoln explained, "Well, whenever one of my generals is licked he says he was outnumbered three or four to one, and we have 400,000 men."

His wit could be bitter. He told the story of a congressman who had been savagely attacked for opposing the War of 1812. When asked to oppose the Mexican War, the old man said, "I opposed one war; that was enough for me. I am now perpetually in favor of war, pestilence, and famine."

As for people who loved to wave the flag, Lincoln would bring up the man who said, "I feel patriotic!" When asked what he meant by that, the man replied, "Why, I feel like I want to kill somebody or steal something."

He could laugh at himself, too. When a political opponent called him "a two-faced man" during a debate, Lincoln replied, "I leave it to my audience. If I had another face, do you think I would wear this one?" He liked to tell the story about the time he was out riding in the woods and met a woman on horseback. As Lincoln paused to let her pass, she reined in, too, and looked sharply at him. "Why, I do believe you are the ugliest man I ever saw," she said. "Madam, you are probably right," he said, "but I can't help it." "No," she said, "you can't help it, but you might stay at home."

Once, when Lincoln was in a courtroom on the circuit, the judge held up a long legal paper drawn up by a notoriously sluggish lawyer. "Astonishing, isn't it, Lincoln?" the judge said. "It's like the lazy preacher who used to write out long sermons," Lincoln replied. "He got to writing and was too lazy to stop."

Leaving town to handle a case, Lincoln hired a horse from a stable. When he brought the horse back a few days later, he asked the stableman, "Keep this horse for funerals?" "No indeed!" replied the owner. "Glad to hear it," Lincoln said, "because if you did, the corpse wouldn't get there in time for the resurrection."

When Lincoln was president, a delegation urged him to appoint one of their cronies commissioner to Hawaii. He was not only a capable man, they said, but he was in delicate health, and the climate there would be good for him. "Gentlemen," said Lincoln, "I am sorry to say that there are eight other applicants for that place, and they are all sicker than your man."

A foreign diplomat dropping in at the White House came across Lincoln polishing his own shoes. "What, Mr. President!" he cried. "You black your own boots?" "Yes," replied Lincoln, "whose do you black?"

Funny stories about the president circulated widely. One he himself especially enjoyed involved two Quaker women who were discussing Lincoln and Jefferson Davis, president of the Confederacy. "I think Jefferson will succeed," said the first woman. "Why does thee think so?" asked the other. "Because Jefferson is a praying man." "And so is Abraham a praying man," said the second. "Yes," said the first, "but the Lord will think Abraham is joking."

In Lincoln's kind of humor there was more than a touch of Mark Twain. The novelist Ernest Hemingway once said, "All modern American literature comes from one book by Mark Twain called *Huckleberry Finn*." Perhaps it really began with Lincoln, who was born a quarter-century earlier and who wrote in the plain, direct language Twain would use many years later.

It was more than humor, of course, that Lincoln (and Twain) strove for in public speech. What Lincoln thought was good writing he described in a eulogy he delivered on the death of the Whig senator Henry Clay, his ideal as a statesman. These words could have been said about Lincoln himself:

Mr. Clay's eloquence did not consist, as many fine specimens of eloquence do, of types and figures—of antithesis and elegant arrangement of words and sentences—but rather of that deeply earnest and impassioned tone and manner, which can proceed only from great sincerity and a thorough conviction in the speaker of the justice and importance of his cause. This it is that truly touches the chords of human sympathy; and those who heard Mr. Clay never failed to be moved by it, or ever afterwards forgot the impression. All his efforts were made for practical effect. He never spoke merely to be heard. . . .

Mr. Clay's predominant sentiment, from first to last, was a deep devotion to the cause of human liberty, a strong sympathy with the oppressed everywhere, and an ardent wish for their elevation. With him this was a primary and all controlling passion. Subsidiary to this was the conduct of his whole life. He loved his country partly because it was his own country, but mostly because it was a free country; and he burned with a zeal for its advancement, prosperity, and glory, because he saw in such, the advancement, prosperity, and glory of human liberty, human right, and human nature. He desired the prosperity of his countrymen partly because they were his countrymen, but chiefly to show to the world that freemen could be prosperous.

6

CAN WE CONTINUE FOREVER—HALF SLAVE AND HALF FREE?

In THE 1850S THE POLITICAL ANTI-slavery movement marched under the banner of Free Speech, Free Soil, and Free Labor. The main aim of most of its followers was to secure the new territories for free white labor. (They had little concern for the interests of blacks, whether free or slave.) They believed that self-help and self-discipline created better workers than the whip that coerced slave labor. Lincoln used himself as an example of the benefits of free labor, of a system that enabled him to rise from a hired hand to a successful lawyer. This principle "that all should have an equal chance," he said, was "the principle that clears the path for all, gives home to all, and, by consequence, enterprise and industry to all."

Thinking about the value of labor, Lincoln set down this note:

In the early days of the world, the Almighty said to the first of our race, "In the sweat of thy face shalt thou eat bread"; and since then, if we except the light and the air of heaven, no good thing has been, or can be enjoyed by us, without having first cost labor. And, inasmuch [as] most good things are produced by labor, it follows that [all] such things of right belong to those whose labor has produced them. But it has so happened in all ages of the world that some have labored, and others have, without labor, enjoyed a large proportion of the fruits. This is wrong and should not continue. To [secure] to each laborer the whole product of his labor, or as nearly as possible, is a most worthy object of any good government.

Later, as president, writing his first annual message to Congress, Lincoln made clear his view of the relationship between labor and capital:

Labor is prior to, and independent of, capital. Capital is only the fruit of labor and could never have existed if labor had not first existed. Labor is the superior of capital and deserves much the higher consideration. Capital has its rights, which are as worthy of protection as any other rights. Nor is it denied that there is, and probably always will be, a relation between labor and capital, producing mutual benefits. The error is in assuming that the whole labor of community exists within that relation. A few men own capital, and that few avoid labor themselves, and, with their capital, hire or buy another few to labor for them. A large majority belong to neither class—neither work for others, nor have others working for them. In most of the Southern states, a majority of the whole people of all colors are neither slaves nor masters; while in the Northern a large majority are neither hirers nor hired. Men with their families—wives, sons, and daughters—work for themselves, on their farms, in their houses, and in their shops, taking the whole product to themselves, and asking no favors of capital on the one hand, nor of hired laborers or slaves on the other. It is not forgotten that a considerable number of persons mingle their own labor with capital— that is, they labor with their own hands and also buy or

> Roger B. Taney <

hire others to labor for them; but this is only a mixed, and not a distinct, class. No people stated is disturbed by the existence of this mixed class.

Again, as has already been said, there is not, of necessity, any such thing as the free hired laborer being fixed to that condition for life. Many independent men everywhere in these states, a few years back in their lives, were hired laborers. The prudent, penniless beginner in the world labors for wages a while, saves a surplus with which to buy tools or land for himself, then labors on his own account another while, and at length hires another new beginner to help him. This is the just and generous and prosperous system, which opens the way to all—gives hope to all, and consequent energy and progress and improvement of condition to all. No men living are more worthy to be trusted than those who toil up from poverty—none less inclined to take, or touch, aught which they have not honestly earned. Let them beware of surrendering a political power which they already possess, and which, if surrendered, will surely be used to close the door of all advancement against such as they and to fix new disabilities and burdens upon them, till all of liberty shall be lost.

By 1850 the political pot was coming to a boil. The Union now had fifteen free and fifteen slave states. Would the new Western territories, acquired by the conquest of Mexico, come in slave or free? California, filling up rapidly with settlers, was the first to seek admission, and as a free state. Many of the free states of the North, defying the law, were refusing to return fugitive slaves to their masters.

A great debate raged over what should be done about these issues. The South threatened disunion unless constitutional protection of slavery was assured. To find a middle ground that he hoped would unite the divided nation, Senator Henry Clay devised a compromise: The territories carved from Mexico would decide the slavery question for themselves. California would come in free. The slave trade in the District of Columbia would be killed, but not slavery itself within the District. And a new and harsher Fugitive Slave Law would be adopted to force Northerners to return runaways to their owners.

That September, after fierce debate in the Congress, Clay's compromise became law. Clay himself admitted it was more a Southern victory than a compromise. But he hoped this would be a final settlement and that peace would now prevail. That was what most Americans wanted to hear, but some knew better. Congressman Thaddeus Stevens of Pennsylvania, a spokesman for the abolitionists, said that this "compromise" would become "the fruitful mother of future rebellion, disunion, and civil war."

What Clay's package of bills did was to overturn the Missouri Compromise of 1820, which had banned slavery in the northern part of the huge territory acquired in the Louisiana Purchase. Now Lincoln and the antislavery people feared slavery would spread into those lands they had believed would remain free soil. An old rival of Lincoln's in Illinois, Senator Stephen Douglas, took the lead in tipping the political balance still further in the South's favor. Lincoln blamed him for playing along with the South to satisfy his intense ambition to be president.

Douglas came up with a scheme to get rid of the slavery issue. He called it "popular sovereignty." Appealing to the American love for self-government, it would allow the people settling in each territory to decide on the status of slavery. With the help of Southern politicians, in 1854 Douglas pushed through Congress a bill creating the new territories of Kansas and Nebraska. It left to the settlers the choice of whether their state government should permit or ban slavery. The law erased the Missouri Compromise line, asserting that the Compromise of 1850 had established majority vote as the new means of dealing with slavery in the territories.

The Douglas law intensified the national crisis. Free Soilers throughout the North raged against it, and people who had once been Whigs or

Democrats split away from their parties over the issue. They cried out that an aggressive slave power had taken over the federal government and was demolishing the hope of freedom for all expressed in the Declaration of Independence. Voters in both the Northern and Midwestern states opposed to "popular sovereignty" began to form a new political party, calling themselves the Republicans. Their aim was to save the Western territories for free labor—for free white men.

While Douglas spoke out in Illinois to defend his Kansas-Nebraska Act, Lincoln, his passion for politics revived, took to the platform to oppose the extension of slavery. Some of his argument is contained in these notes he prepared sometime in 1854:

Although volume upon volume is written to prove slavery a very good thing, we never hear of the man who wishes to take the good of it, by being a slave himself.

Most governments have been based, practically, on the denial of equal rights of men; ours began by affirming those rights. They said, some men are too ignorant and vicious to share in government. Possibly so, said we; and, by your system, you would always keep them ignorant and vicious. We proposed to give all a chance; and we expected the weak to grow stronger, the ignorant, wiser; and all better, and happier together. . . .

If A can prove, however conclusively, that he may, of right, enslave B—why may not B snatch the same argument, and prove equally, that he may enslave A?

You say A is white, and B is black. It is color, then, the lighter having the right to enslave the darker? Take care. By this rule you are to be slave to the first man you meet with a fairer skin than your own.

You do not mean color exactly? You mean the whites are intellectually the superiors of the blacks and, therefore, have the right to enslave them? Take care again. By this rule, you are to be slave to the first man you meet with an intellect superior to your own.

But, say you, it is a question of interest; and, if you can make it your interest, you have the right to enslave another. Very well. And if he can make it his interest, he has the right to enslave you.

In Peoria, Illinois, on October 16, 1854, Lincoln gave a long speech presenting the moral case against slavery. He was trying to show why scrapping the Missouri Compromise was wrong, for the direct effect would be to let slavery into Kansas and Nebraska. The very principle of "popular sovereignty" meant allowing slavery to spread wherever people might be inclined to take it:

This declared indifference but, as I must think, covert real zeal for the spread of slavery, I cannot but hate. I hate it because it deprives our republican example of its just influence in the world—enables the enemies of free institutions, with plausibility, to taunt us as hypocrites—causes the real friends of freedom to doubt our sincerity, and especially because it forces so many really good men amongst ourselves into an open war with the very fundamental principles of civil liberty—criticizing the Declaration of Independence and insisting that there is no right principle of action but self-interest. . . .

I trust I understand and truly estimate the right of self-government. My faith in the proposition that each man should do precisely as he pleases with all which is exclusively his own, lies at the foundation of the sense of justice there is in me. I extend the principles to communities of men, as well as to individuals. I so extend it, because it is politically

wise, as well as naturally just: politically wise, in saving us from broils about matters which do not concern us. Here, or at Washington, I would not trouble myself with the oyster laws of Virginia or the cranberry laws of Indiana.

The doctrine of self-government is right—absolutely and eternally right—but it has no just application as here attempted. Or perhaps I should rather say that whether it has such just application depends upon whether a Negro is not or is a man. If he is not a man, why in that case, he who is a man may, as a matter of self-government, do just as he pleases with him. But if the Negro is a man, is it not to that extent a total destruction of self-government to say that he, too, shall not govern himself? When the white man governs himself, that is self-government; but when he governs himself and also governs another man, that is more than self-government—that is despotism. If the Negro is a man, why then my ancient faith teaches me that "all men are created equal" and that there can be no moral right in connection with one man's making a slave of another. . . .

Near eighty years ago we began by declaring that all men are created equal; but now from that beginning we have run down to the other declaration, that for some men to enslave others is a "sacred right of self-government." These principles cannot stand together. They are as opposite as God and Mammon; and whoever holds to the one, must despise the other. . . .

Let no one be deceived. The spirit of Seventy-six and the spirit of Nebraska are utter antagonisms; and the former is being rapidly displaced by the latter. . . .

Fellow countrymen—Americans south as well as north—shall we make no effort to arrest this? Already the liberal throughout the world express the apprehension "that the one retrograde institution in America is undermining the principles of progress and fatally violating the noblest political system the world ever saw." This is not the taunt of enemies but the warning of friends. Is it quite safe to disregard it—to despise it? Is there no danger to liberty itself, in discarding the earliest practice and first precept of our ancient faith? In our greedy chase to make profit of the Negro, let us beware lest we "cancel and tear to pieces" even the white man's charter of freedom.

Our republican robe is soiled and trailed in the dust. Let us repurify it. Let us turn and wash it white, in the spirit, if not the blood, of the Revolution. Let us turn slavery from its claims of "moral right," back upon its existing legal rights and its arguments of "necessity." Let us return it to the position our fathers gave it; and there let it rest in peace. Let us re-adopt the Declaration of Independence, and with it the practices and policy which harmonize with it. Let North and South—let all Americans—let all lovers of liberty everywhere—join in the great and good work. If we do this, we shall not only have saved the Union; but we shall have so saved it, as to make it, and to keep it, forever worthy of the saving. We shall have so saved it that the succeeding millions of free happy people, the world over, shall rise up and call us blessed to the latest generations.

Many Americans, including some Southerners, believed in—or rather, hoped for—the gradual disappearance of slavery. Give it time and it would simply fade away. A Kentucky judge who expressed that confidence in a book, sent a copy to Lincoln. In his thank-you letter Lincoln challenged that belief:

You spoke of "the peaceful extinction of slavery" and used other expressions indicating your belief that the thing was, at some time, to have an end. Since then we have had thirty-six years of experience; and this experience has demonstrated, I think, that there is no peaceful extinction of slavery in prospect for us. The signal failure of Henry Clay and other good and great men, in 1849, to effect anything in favor of gradual emancipation in Kentucky, together with a thousand other signs, extinguishes that hope utterly. On the question of liberty, as a principle, we are not what we have been. When we were the political slaves of King George and wanted to be free, we called the maxim that "all men are created equal" a self-evident truth; but now when we have grown fat and have lost all dread of being slaves ourselves, we have become so greedy to be masters that we call the same maxim "a self-evident lie." The Fourth of July has not quite dwindled away; it is still a great day—for burning firecrackers!

That spirit, which desired the peaceful extinction of slavery, has itself become extinct with the occasion and the men of the Revolution. Under the impulse of that occasion, nearly half the states adopted systems of emancipation at once; and it is a significant fact that not a single state has done the like since. So far as peaceful voluntary emancipation is concerned, the condition of the Negro slave in America, scarcely less terrible to the contemplation of a free mind, is now so fixed and hopeless of change for the better as that of the lost souls of the finally impenitent. The autocrat of all the Russians will resign his crown and proclaim his subjects free republicans sooner than will our American masters voluntarily give up their slaves.

Our political problem now is, "Can we, as a nation, continue together permanently—forever—half slave and half free?" The problem is too mighty for me. May God, in His mercy, superintend the solution.

A few days later, Lincoln wrote another letter on slavery, this time to his closest friend, Joshua Speed, a Kentuckian with whom Lincoln had once roomed. The letter also denounces the nativist American Party (called the "Know-Nothings" by its detractors), which opposed letting immigrants and Catholics vote or hold office:

You know I dislike slavery, and you fully admit the abstract wrong of it. So far there is no cause of difference. But you say that sooner than yield your legal right to the slave—especially at the bidding of those who are not themselves interested—you would see the Union dissolved. I am not aware that anyone is bidding you to yield that right; very certainly I am not. I leave that matter entirely to yourself. I also acknowledge your rights and my obligations under the Constitution in regard to your slaves. I confess I hate to see the poor creatures hunted down and caught and carried back to their stripes and unrewarded toils; but I bite my lip and keep quiet. In 1841 you and I had together a tedious low-water trip on a steamboat from Louisville to St. Louis. You may remember, as I well do, that from Louisville to the mouth of the Ohio, there were on board ten or a dozen slaves, shackled together with irons. That sight was a continual torment to me; and I see something like it every time I touch the Ohio, or any other slave border. It is hardly fair for you to assume that I have no interest in a thing which has, and continually exercises, the power of making me miserable. You ought rather to appreciate how much the great body of the Northern people do crucify their feelings in order to maintain their loyalty to the Constitution and the Union. . . .

I am not a Know-Nothing. That is certain. How could I be? How can anyone who abhors the oppression of Negroes be in favor of degrading classes of white people? Our progress in degeneracy appears to me to be pretty rapid. As a nation, we began by declaring that "all men are created equal." We now practically read it "all men are created equal, except Negroes." When the Know-Nothings get control, it will read "All men are created equal, except Negroes, and foreigners, and Catholics." When it comes to this I prefer emigrating to some country where they make no pretense of loving liberty—to Russia, for instance, where despotism can be taken pure and without the base alloy of hypocrisy.

In the spring of 1855 Kansas became the cockpit of civil war between proslavery and antislavery settlers. Dual governments were set up. One was dominated by armed men in from Missouri, who were called "Border Ruffians." They enacted laws protecting slavery. The other was the creation of settlers from New England bound to make Kansas free soil. Fighting broke out in 1856 between guerrillas from both sides.

"Bleeding Kansas" became the chief political issue in the 1856 presidential contest. The fierce struggle probably cost Douglas the Democratic nomination for president. His party chose James Buchanan of Pennsylvania instead, but it still backed "popular sovereignty" in its platform. The Republicans nominated John C. Frémont, the Western explorer, and made "Free Soil, Free Speech, and Frémont" their slogan. Lincoln gave some fifty speeches in Illinois for Frémont. He had his mind set on challenging Douglas for the Senate in 1858, and this ardent campaigning wouldn't hurt.

When Buchanan won the election, he advised the nation that this "long agitation" over the constitutional issue of slavery would soon be settled by a decision of the Supreme Court. He counseled the country to bow to the decision, "whatever it might be."

He was talking about the Dred Scott case, which had been before the court for years. Dred Scott, a slave, had been taken by his master from the slave state of Missouri to the free state of Illinois and then to the Wisconsin Territory, where slavery was banned by the Missouri Compromise. Scott sued for his liberty, holding that he had become free because of his long stay on free soil. The case finally reached the Supreme Court. Two days after Buchanan's inaugural, Chief Justice Roger B. Taney handed down a crushing blow to the position of Dred Scott and all African-Americans. He held that blacks had long been considered "beings of an inferior order and altogether unfit to associate with the white race, either socially or politically, and so far inferior that they had no rights which the white man was bound to respect."

Biting even deeper, Taney ruled that "Congress had no power to abolish or prevent slavery in any of the territories." He was saying that the Missouri Compromise had never been constitutional.

The Taney decision outraged the Republicans. Even Democrats admitted it was politically motivated. Racists were jubilant: the Supreme Court had enshrined white supremacy.

Douglas spoke out in support of the Taney decision. Lincoln thought the ruling was a giant step toward nationalizing slavery. He studied the court's action and collected editorials and speeches on both sides of the issue as he prepared a carefully reasoned attack upon the Dred Scott ruling. He showed how the condition of African-Americans had worsened as the years passed. On June 26, 1857, he spoke in the state capital at Springfield:

The Chief Justice does not directly assert, but plainly assumes, as a fact, that the public estimate of the black

man is more favorable now than it was in the days of Revolution. This assumption is a mistake. In some trifling particulars, the condition of that race has been ameliorated; but, as a whole in this country, the change between then and now is decidedly the other way; and their ultimate destiny has never appeared so hopeless as in the last three or four years. In two of the five states—New Jersey and North Carolina—that then gave the free Negro the right of voting, the right has since been taken away; and in a third—New York—it has been greatly abridged; while it has not been extended, so far as I know, to a single additional state, though the number of states has more than doubled. In those days, as I understand, masters could, at their own pleasure, emancipate their slaves; but since then, such legal restraints have been made upon emancipation as to amount almost to prohibition. In those days, legislatures held the unquestioned power to abolish slavery in their respective states; but now it is becoming quite fashionable for state constitutions to withhold that power from the legislatures. In those days, by common consent, the spread of the black man's bondage to new countries was prohibited; but now, Congress decides that it will not continue the prohibition, and the Supreme Court decides that it could not if it would. In those days, our Declaration of Independence was held sacred by all, and thought to include all; but now, to aid in making the bondage of the Negro universal and eternal, it is assailed and sneered at, and construed and hawked at, and torn till, if its framers could rise from their graves, they could not at all recognize it. . . .

I think the authors of that notable instrument intended to include all men, but they did not intend to declare all men equal in all respects. They did not mean to say all were equal in color, size, intellect, moral developments, or social capacity. They defined with tolerable distinctness, in what respects they did consider all men created equal—equal in "certain inalienable rights, among which are life, liberty, and the pursuit of happiness." This they said, and this [they] meant. They did not mean to assert the obvious untruth, that all were then actually enjoying that equality, nor yet, that they were about to confer it immediately upon them. In fact they had no power to confer such a boon. They meant simply to declare the right, so that the enforcement of it might follow as fast as circumstances should permit. They meant to set up a standard maxim for free society, which should be familiar to all and revered by all; constantly looked to, constantly labored for, and even though never perfectly attained, constantly approximated, and thereby constantly spreading and deepening its influence and augmenting the happiness and value of life to all people of all colors everywhere. The assertion that "all men are created equal" was of no practical use in effecting our separation from Great Britain; and it was placed in the Declaration, not for that, but for future use. Its authors meant it to be—thank God, it is now proving itself—a stumbling block to those who in after times might seek to turn a free people back into the hateful paths of despotism. They knew the proneness of prosperity to breed tyrants, and they meant when such should reappear in this fair land and commence their vocation they should find left for them at least one hard nut to crack.

Soon after this, Lincoln began to draft a speech, which built to the biblical warning in Matthew and Mark about a house divided. It included these notes on self-government:

Well, I, too, believe in self-government as I understand it; but I do not understand that the privilege one man takes of making a slave of another, or holding him as such, is any part of "self-government." To call it so is, to my mind, simply absurd and ridiculous. I am for the people of the whole nation doing just as they please in all matters which concern the whole nation; for those of each part doing just as they choose in all matters which concern no other part; and for each individual doing just as he chooses in all matters which concern nobody else.

This is the principle. Of course I am content with any exception which the Constitution, or the actually existing state of things, makes a necessity. But neither the principle nor the exception will admit the indefinite spread and perpetuity of human slavery.

He was preparing the political and moral ground for the long struggle to take over Douglas's seat in the Senate.

7

THE GREAT STRUGGLE BETWEEN TWO PRINCIPLES

As the summer of 1858 came on, the Illinois Republicans met in Springfield and unanimously nominated Lincoln for the U.S. Senate. The Democrats had already chosen Stephen Douglas to be their candidate for another term. Up to this moment Lincoln had won office five times. He had served in the state legislature for four terms and in the Congress for one. This he followed with ten years of private life and his law practice. It was the Kansas-Nebraska Act that drew him back into politics. Why did he choose to run for the Senate now? He gave the answer himself:

Allow me now, in my own way, to state with what aims and objects I did enter upon this campaign. I claim no extraordinary exemption from personal ambition. That I like preferment as well as the average of men may be admitted. But I protest I have not entered upon this hard contest solely, or even chiefly, for a mere personal object. I clearly see, as I think, a powerful plot to make slavery universal and perpetual in this nation. The effort to carry that plot through will be persistent and long continued, extending far beyond the senatorial term for which Judge Douglas and I are just now struggling. I enter upon the contest to contribute my humble and temporary mite in opposition to that effort.

On the night he was nominated—June 16, 1858—Lincoln spoke to the convention on the theme of "a house divided." Before the speech, it was mainly the people of the Midwest who knew his name. This speech, however, won front-page attention in newspapers far beyond Illinois. Some listeners and readers thought it a radical message that might be taken as a call for war, although Lincoln carefully kept from attacking the slaveholders themselves. Here are his opening lines:

> If we could first know where we are and whither we are tending, we could then better judge what to do and how to do it.
>
> We are now far into the fifth year since a policy was initiated with the avowed object, and confident promise, of putting an end to slavery agitation.
>
> Under the operation of that policy, that agitation has not only not ceased, but has constantly augmented.
>
> In my opinion, it will not cease until a crisis shall have been reached and passed.
>
> "A house divided against itself cannot stand."
>
> I believe this government cannot endure, permanently, half slave and half free.
>
> I do not expect the Union to be dissolved—I do not expect the house to fall—but I do expect it will cease to be divided.
>
> It will become all one thing, or all the other.
>
> Either the opponents of slavery will arrest the further spread of it and place it where the public mind shall rest in the belief that it is in course of ultimate extinction; or

>Stephen A. Douglas<

its advocates will push it forward, till it shall become alike lawful in all states—old as well as new, North as well as South.

Lincoln thought he had a good chance to beat Douglas, for Northern Democrats had deserted to the Republicans over free soil. On the advice of party leaders, Lincoln followed Douglas around the state. He spoke in many of the same towns Douglas did. Although they did not yet meet face-to-face, in effect it was a debate on the issue of slavery.

At the root of Lincoln's thinking was the Declaration of Independence. Again and again in his speeches, he raised the principles Jefferson had voiced so eloquently. And with the power of his own voice, Lincoln helps us to understand what it is about the American dream that draws immigrants the world over to these shores:

We are now a mighty nation, we are thirty—or about thirty—millions of people and we own and inhabit about one-fifteenth part of the dry land of the whole earth. We run our memory back over the pages of history for about eighty-two years, and we discover that we were then a very small people in point of numbers, vastly inferior to what we are now, with a vastly less extent of country, with vastly less of everything we deem desirable among men. We look upon the change as exceedingly advantageous to us and to our posterity, and we fix upon something that happened a way back, as in some way or other being connected with this rise of prosperity.

We find a race of men living in that day whom we claim as our fathers and grandfathers; they were iron men; they fought for the principle that they were contending for; and we understood that by what they then did it has followed that the degree of prosperity that we now enjoy has come to us. We hold this annual celebration [Independence Day] to remind ourselves of all the good done in this process of time, of how it was done and who did it, and how we are historically connected with it; and we go from these meetings in better humor with ourselves—we feel more attached the one to the other and more firmly bound to the country we inhabit. In every way we are better men in the age and race and country in which we live for these celebrations.

But after we have done all this we have not yet reached the whole. There is something else connected with it. We have besides these men—descended by blood from our ancestors—among us perhaps half our people who are not descendants at all of these men; they are men who have come from Europe—German, Irish, French, and Scandinavian—men that have come from Europe themselves, or whose ancestors have come hither and settled here, finding themselves our equals in all things. If they look back through this history to trace their connection with those days by blood, they find they have none, they cannot carry themselves back into that glorious epoch and make themselves feel that they are part of us. But when they look through that old Declaration of Independence they find that those old men say that "we hold these truths to be self-evident, that all men are created equal," and then they feel that that moral sentiment taught in that day evidences their relation to those men, that it is the father of all moral principle in them, and that they have a right to claim it as though they were blood of the blood, and flesh of the flesh, of the men who wrote the Declaration, and so they are. That is the electric cord in that Declaration that links the

hearts of patriotic and liberty-loving men together, that will link those patriotic hearts as long as the love of freedom exists in the mind of men throughout the world. . . .

This argument of the judge is the same old serpent that says you work and I eat, you toil and I will enjoy the fruits of it. Turn it whatever way you will—whether it come from the mouth of a king, an excuse for enslaving the people of his country, or from the mouth of men of one race as a reason for enslaving the men of another race, it is all the same old serpent, and I hold if that course of argumentation that is made for the purpose of convincing the public mind that we should not care about this should be granted, it does not stop with the Negro. I should like to know if taking this old Declaration of Independence, which declares that all men are equal upon principle, and making exceptions to it, where will it stop? If one man says it does not mean a Negro, why may not another say it does not mean some other man?

A week later Lincoln talked about slavery and his understanding of the words "all men are created equal":

My declarations upon this subject of Negro slavery may be misrepresented but cannot be misunderstood. I have said that I do not understand the Declaration to mean that all men were created equal in all respects. They are not our equal in color; but I suppose that it does mean to declare that all men are created equal in some respects; they are equal in their right to "life, liberty, and the pursuit of happiness." Certainly the Negro is not our equal in color— perhaps not in many other respects; still, in the right to put into his mouth the bread that his own hands have earned, he is the equal of every other man, white or black. In pointing out that more has been given you, you can not be justified in taking away the little which has been given him. All I ask for the Negro is that if you do not like him, let him alone. If God gave him but little, that little let him enjoy.

About a month later, hearing that Douglas had offered to "fight" him, Lincoln delighted a crowd with this response:

I am informed that my distinguished friend yesterday became a little excited—nervous, perhaps—and he said something about fighting, as though referring to a pugilistic encounter between him and myself. Did anybody in this audience hear him use such language? [Cries of yes.] I am informed, further, that somebody in his audience, rather more excited, or nervous, than himself, took off his coat and offered to take the job off Judge Douglas's hands and fight Lincoln himself. Did anybody here witness that warlike proceeding? [Laughter, and cries of yes.] Well, I merely desire to say that I shall fight neither Judge Douglas nor his second. [Great laughter.] I shall not do this for two reasons, which I will now explain. In the first place, a fight would prove nothing which is in issue in this contest. It might establish that Judge Douglas is a more muscular man than myself, or it might demonstrate that I am a more muscular man than Judge Douglas. But this question is not referred to in the Cincinnati platform, nor in either of the Springfield platforms. [Great laughter.] Neither result would prove him right or me wrong. And so of the gentleman who volunteered to do his fighting for him. If my fighting Judge Douglas would not prove anything, it would certainly prove nothing for me to fight his bottle-holder. [Continued laughter.]

My second reason for not having a personal encounter with the Judge is that I don't believe he wants it himself. [Laughter.] He and I are about the best friends in the world, and when we get together he would no more think of fighting me than of fighting his wife. Therefore, ladies and gentlemen, when the judge talked about fighting, he was not giving vent to any ill-feeling of his own but merely trying to excite enthusiasm against me on the part of his audience. And as I find he was tolerably successful, we will call it quits.

When members of the Continental Congress adopted the Declaration of Independence on July 4, 1776, did they mean that it should apply to all God's creatures—or only to some? Lincoln gave his opinion to a crowd of six thousand standing in the public square at Lewistown, Illinois:

These communities, by their representatives in old Independence Hall, said to the whole world of men: "We hold these truths to be self-evident: that all men are created equal; that they are endowed by their Creator with certain unalienable rights; that among these are life, liberty, and the pursuit of happiness." This was their majestic interpretation of the economy of the universe. This was their lofty and wise and noble understanding of the justice of the Creator to His creatures. Yes, gentlemen, to all His creatures, to the whole great family of man. In their enlightened belief, nothing stamped with the divine image and likeness was sent into the world to be trodden on and degraded and imbruted by its fellows. They grasped not only the whole race of man then living, but they reached forward and seized upon the farthest posterity. They erected a beacon to guide their children and their children's children, and the countless myriads who should inhabit the earth in other ages. Wise statesmen as they were, they knew the tendency of prosperity to breed tyrants, and so they established these great self-evident truths, that when in the distant future some man, some faction, some interest, should set up the doctrine that none but rich men, or none but white men, were entitled to life, liberty, and the pursuit of happiness, their posterity might look up again to the Declaration of Independence and take courage to renew the battle which their fathers began—so that truth and justice and mercy, and all the humane and Christian virtues, might not be extinguished from the land; so that no man would hereafter dare to limit and circumscribe the great principles on which the temple of liberty was built.

Late in August, the two candidates for the U.S. Senate began to meet in formal debate, standing on the same platform. In the small towns of Illinois the debates provided grand entertainment. As many as fifteen thousand people came from all corners of the state to stand in a hot sun and revel in hours of oratory. By the end of the debates Lincoln's carefully researched and crafted speeches had won him a national reputation.

In their final debate, Lincoln and Douglas met at Alton—the town where the antislavery editor Elijah Lovejoy was lynched. Lincoln charged that the Democrats had never admitted there was anything wrong with slavery, and he went on to say in half-a-dozen sentences what the true issue confronting the country was:

It is the eternal struggle between these two principles —right and wrong—throughout the world. They are the two principles that have stood face-to-face from the beginning of time and will ever continue to struggle. The one is

the common right of humanity and the other the divine right of kings. It is the same principle in whatever shape it develops itself. It is the same spirit that says, "You work and toil and earn bread, and I'll eat it." No matter in what shape it comes, whether from the mouth of a king who seeks to bestride the people of his own nation and live by the fruit of their labor, or from one race of men as an apology for enslaving another race, it is the same tyrannical principle.

Lincoln had a way of putting things tersely and pungently. He hit home on slavery with these remarks:

I have always thought that all men should be free; but if any should be slaves it should be first those who desire it for themselves, and secondly, those who desire it for others. Whenever I hear anyone arguing for slavery, I feel a strong impulse to see it tried on him personally.

As I would not be a slave, so I would not be a master. This expresses my idea of democracy. Whatever differs from this, to the extent of the difference, is no democracy.

He who would be no slave, must consent to have no slave. Those who deny freedom to others deserve it not for themselves; and under a just God, cannot long retain it.

And again, commenting on the claim of an Alabama minister that slavery was ordained by God, and therefore a good thing, Lincoln said:

Slavery is good for some people! As a good thing, slavery is strikingly peculiar, in this, that it is the only good thing which no man ever seeks the good of for himself.

The most famous debates in American history revealed the deep differences between the Republican and the Democratic views on slavery. Douglas kept saying he did not care whether slavery was voted up or down. Lincoln, on the other hand, held that slavery was a moral, social, and political evil. Yet what he said in the debates showed his ambivalence. While the Republicans opposed slavery, they did not believe fully in racial equality. And as evil as slavery was, Lincoln's party did not intend to interfere with it in the South, where it existed; they only wished to prevent its expansion.

Why didn't the Republicans demand action to end slavery here and now in the states where it existed? Because slavery could not have been abolished peacefully except by an amendment to the Constitution that would permit the federal government to legislate on a matter that was reserved to the decision of the individual states. To win such an amendment would require a two-thirds majority of both houses of Congress and then, for its ratification, a majority of three-fourths of the states' legislatures. That would have been impossible against the resistance of the fifteen slave states.

This is why Lincoln and the Republicans kept saying they were not attacking the legal status of slavery; they knew how hard that would be to do away with. They felt they had to limit their campaign to keeping slavery out of the territories, in the hope it would eventually die.

In the elections to the state legislature that fall of 1858, the Republicans got slightly more votes than the Democrats. But Douglas people carried the counties, which preserved the Democratic majority in the legislature. The result was the reelection of Douglas to the Senate. (In those times senators were chosen not by popular ballot but by the state legislatures.) In the North, generally, the Democrats lost badly. If the Republicans continued to do as well in 1860, they could win the presidency. And if that should happen, threatened some fiery Southerners, then the slave states must secede from the Union.

8

LET US
HAVE FAITH
THAT RIGHT
MAKES MIGHT

It HURT TO LOSE THAT ELECTION. "I feel like the boy who stumped his toe," Lincoln said. "I am too big to cry and too badly hurt to laugh." Yet, a few days later, he wrote a friend:

> Of course I wished, but I did not much expect a better result. . . . I am glad I made the late race. It gave me a hearing on the great and durable questions of the age, which I could have had in no other way; and although I now sink out of view and shall be forgotten, I believe I have made some marks which will tell for the cause of civil liberty long after I am gone.

Again Lincoln returned to his law practice. He earned good fees as counsel to railroad corporations, and soon he had built a comfortable income. Powerful Republicans in the East began talking about him as a good bet for the presidency. They liked his moderate views; other men whose eyes were on the White House—like Senators William Seward of New York and Salmon Chase of Ohio—were feared as too radical. When a Republican editor pushed Lincoln to announce his candidacy, Lincoln replied, "I do not think myself fit for the presidency." He knew he had no administrative experience and detested the burdens of office that went with an executive post. No, he would rather use his gift of eloquence for debate in the Senate. Maybe he'd take on Douglas again in 1864.

Meanwhile, as a loyal Republican he did his best to build the party—and his own standing. He had the debates with Douglas printed up in a booklet and distributed nationally. In letter after letter he kept in touch with party leaders beyond his state, offering advice on strategy and tactics. And he spoke two dozen times to audiences throughout the Midwest.

North and South moved rapidly toward a showdown in October 1859, when John Brown and eighteen men—five of them African-Americans—attacked the federal arsenal at Harpers Ferry, Virginia. They planned to seize the weapons stored there, free the slaves in the vicinity, and retreat into the Alleghenies. There they meant to fortify a base from which to encourage and aid slave uprisings. Eventually all the slaves would join, they thought, and slavery would be doomed.

It was a hopeless mission—a handful against overwhelming white power. U.S. troops under Colonel Robert E. Lee stifled the threat easily. Most members of the band were captured, and Brown himself, wounded, was quickly tried for treason, convicted, and sentenced to death. Just before hanging he uttered these prophetic words:

> *You may dispose of me very easily; I am nearly disposed of now. But this question is still to be settled—this Negro question, I mean; the end of that is not yet. You had better—all you people at the South—prepare yourselves for a settlement of this question.*

Though it failed, Brown's raid shook the nation. To Southern leaders it was final proof of the North's violent intentions. While many in the North rejected Brown's tactics, they praised his devotion to freedom for the slave. To the abolitionists and to African-Americans both slave and free, he became a revolutionary martyr.

John Brown

Most Republican leaders hastily condemned Brown's attack and called him a fanatic. Their party had never advocated slave insurrection or invasion of the South. Maybe Brown was crazed by his devotion to abolition, thought Lincoln, but as he learned more about the man he came to respect his great courage. The day after Brown's execution Lincoln said that thinking slavery was wrong did not justify violence and treason. But he warned the South that "if constitutionally we elect a president, and therefore you undertake to destroy the Union, it will be our duty to deal with you as old John Brown has been dealt with."

A few months later, Lincoln answered the Southern charge that the Republicans were to blame for Harpers Ferry. He also made clear why large-scale slave revolts were so unlikely:

Some of you admit that no Republican designedly aided or encouraged the Harpers Ferry affair but still insist that our doctrines and declarations necessarily lead to such results. We do not believe it. We know we hold to no doctrine, and make no declaration, which were not held to and made by "our fathers who framed the government under which we live."

Republican doctrines and declarations are accompanied with a continual protest against any interference whatever with your slaves, or with you about your slaves. Surely, this does not encourage them to revolt. True, we do, in common with "our fathers, who framed the government under which we live," declare our belief that slavery is wrong; but the slaves do not hear us declare even this. For anything we say or do, the slaves would scarcely know there is a Republican Party. I believe they would not, in fact, generally know it but for your misrepresentations of us in their hearing.

100

In your political contests slave insurrections are not more common now than they were before the Republican Party was organized. What induced the Southampton insurrection twenty-eight years ago [slave insurrection of 1831, led by Nat Turner, in Southampton County, Virginia], in which at least three times as many lives were lost as at Harpers Ferry? You can scarcely stretch your very elastic fancy to the conclusion that Southampton was "got up by Black Republicanism." In the present state of things in the United States, I do not think a general, or even a very extensive slave insurrection, is possible. The indispensable concert of action cannot be attained. The slaves have no means of rapid communication; nor can incendiary freemen, black or white, supply it. The explosive materials are everywhere in parcels, but there neither are, nor can be supplied, the indispensable connecting trains.

Early in 1860 Lincoln agreed to let his political friends launch a "Lincoln for President" movement. It would not be easy going, for even in his own state some Republicans were divided over him. Was he too liberal? Too inexperienced? Wouldn't other men be better choices? Lincoln tried hard to mediate disputes within the Illinois party, winning support as the favorite-son candidate. Late that winter he went to New York to give an important speech at Cooper Union, where Eastern bigwigs and the press would stand in judgment. He was greeted as a celebrity and had a campaign photograph taken at Mathew Brady's famous studio. Now fifty-one, he stood erect, dressed in a new black suit, and with his left hand resting on a pile of books, presented to the nation the image of a confident statesman.

On the night of February 27, 1860, he spoke to fifteen hundred people gathered, despite a snowstorm, in the great hall. Drawing upon thorough research, he demonstrated that the Founding Fathers had exercised their constitutional right in excluding slavery from the territories, counter to what Douglas claimed. He criticized the Southerners' refusal to permit open discussion of slavery and their censorship of news of the Republican Party's views. In this closing passage he took up the moral issue facing the nation:

If slavery is right, all words, acts, laws, and constitutions against it are themselves wrong, and should be silenced and swept away. If it is right, we cannot justly object to its nationality—its universality. If it is wrong, they cannot justly insist upon its extension—its enlargement. All they ask, we could readily grant, if we thought slavery right; all we ask, they could as readily grant, if they thought it wrong. Their thinking it right and our thinking it wrong is the precise fact upon which depends the whole controversy. Thinking it right, as they do, they are not to blame for desiring its full recognition as being right; but, thinking it wrong, as we do, can we yield to them? Can we cast our votes with their view and against our own? In view of our moral, social, and political responsibilities, can we do this?

Wrong as we think slavery is, we can yet afford to let it alone where it is, because that much is due to the necessity arising from its actual presence in the nation; but can we, while our votes will prevent it, allow it to spread into the national territories and to overrun us here in these free states? If our sense of duty forbids this, then let us stand by our duty, fearlessly and effectively. Let us be diverted by none of those sophistical contrivances wherewith we are so industriously plied and belabored—contrivances such as groping for some middle ground between the right and the wrong, vain as the search for a man who should be neither a living man nor a dead man; such as a policy of "don't care" on a question about which all true men do care, such as Union appeals beseeching true Union men to yield to Disunionists, reversing the divine rule, and calling, not the sinners, but the righteous to repentance; such as invocations to Washington, imploring men to unsay what Washington said and undo what Washington did.

Neither let us be slandered from our duty by false accusations against us, nor frightened from it by menaces of destruction to the government nor of dungeons to ourselves. Let us have faith that right makes might, and in that faith, let us, to the end, dare to do our duty as we understand it.

That speech won him a standing ovation and considerably advanced his candidacy among Eastern Republicans. Many papers printed it in full. He returned to Springfield, waiting there while the Republican National Convention met in Chicago. On May 18, on the third ballot, he was nominated for president.

9

A NEW PRESIDENT: THE SOUTH SECEDES

LINCOLN ENTERED THE 1860 RACE
for the presidency with many advantages. He came from a key section
and a key state. He had renounced slavery as a moral evil but assured
everyone he would not interfere with it in the South. He had solid experience in politics as a legislator but had not served long enough to make
many enemies. His public image as "Honest Abe" and the "Railsplitter"
had great appeal. His debates with Douglas and his other speeches proved
he was highly intelligent and movingly eloquent.

His opposition was badly split. The Democrats couldn't agree on a
single platform and candidate, so their party broke in two, one in the
North and one in the South. A third party made a hasty appearance to
gather the votes of old Whig and Know-Nothing diehards, hoping to delay
action on the slavery issue still longer.

The Republican platform was short and solid. It stood against the
expansion of slavery. It opposed any changes in naturalization laws that
might injure the rights of immigrants. It called for a homestead act to
promote agricultural expansion westward, and for government aid to improve rivers and harbors and build a transcontinental railroad. Those
planks appealed successfully to a broad spectrum of voters.

In the slave states the prospect of a Republican president caused
mass hysteria. Many suspected of inciting slave revolts were whipped,
tarred and feathered, or lynched. Hundreds of Northern whites were or-

dered to quit the South or face death. The scare stories were false, but they built a climate of almost unbearable fear. The political leaders and state legislators threatened secession if Lincoln was elected.

Lincoln kept a low profile during the campaign. Presidential candidates in that time did not race around the country making speeches in their own behalf. And because he was seeking the vote of many groups often disagreeing on some points, it was safer to be silent and avoid displeasing anyone. While he stayed quietly at home, Republicans campaigned for him throughout the North. As is usually the case, they stressed whatever issues appealed to the particular region. But they always insisted that their party would not interfere with slavery in the South.

The outcome? The North and West went Republican, rolling up 54 percent of the total popular vote in that region, while Douglas's Northern Democrats got most of the rest. Lincoln got no votes in the South, where his name did not even appear on the ballot. The slave states went heavily to John Breckinridge, candidate of the Southern Democrats, with John Bell of the small third party trailing behind. Lincoln won a plurality of 40 percent of the popular vote but a majority of the electoral votes and was elected president. Republicans rejoiced that "the country has once and for all thrown off the domination of the slaveholders."

In that time presidents did not take office in January as they now do, but in March. In that long interval, the Democrat James Buchanan remained in the White House. He proved to be helpless as in the South state after state voted for secession. So rapidly did they move that, by the time Lincoln took office, eleven Southern states had seceded, established a government they called the Confederate States of America, and elected Jefferson Davis of Mississippi as its president.

The events signaled the beginning of the Second American Revolution, as some have called it. By seceding from the United States, the Southerners proclaimed that they refused to become a permanent minority in the nation, suffering a loss of political power that would ruin the institution of slavery and the society upon which it was built.

Jefferson Davis

In the North many merchants, manufacturers, and bankers feared independence would cripple business. Working people, too, worried that bad economic conditions could bring about mass unemployment. Those grave concerns and the general dread of war led to calls for compromise with the South, for peace at almost any price. While Lincoln waited for his term to begin, constitutional amendments were proposed that would allow the expansion of slavery. Lincoln secretly advised Republican congressmen to make no such concessions. The Republican rank-and-file rallied behind that view by flooding Congress with letters demanding it remain true to free-soil principles and reject compromise.

On February 11, 1861, Lincoln began his long, slow journey to Washington. From the back of the train pulling out of Springfield, he said this brief good-bye to his neighbors:

My friends:

No one, not in my situation, can appreciate my feeling of sadness at this parting. To this place, and the kindness of these people, I owe everything. Here I have lived a quarter of a century and have passed from a young to an old man. Here my children have been born, and one is buried. I now leave, not knowing when, or whether ever, I may return, with a task before me greater than that which rested upon Washington. Without the assistance of that Divine Being, who ever attended him, I cannot succeed. With that assistance I cannot fail. Trusting in Him, who can go with me and remain with you and be everywhere for good, let us confidently hope that all will yet be well. To His care commending you, as I hope in your prayers you will commend me, I bid you an affectionate farewell.

Again and again on his way to Washington, Lincoln was obliged to make some remarks to the gathering crowds about what lay ahead for the nation. He tried not to worsen the tension and to be reassuring. At Indianapolis he said the nation's fate depended upon the people:

> I will only say that to the salvation of this Union there needs but one single thing—the hearts of a people like yours. When the people rise in masses in behalf of the Union and the liberties of their country, truly may it be said, "The gates of hell shall not prevail against them."
>
> In all the trying positions in which I shall be placed, and doubtless I shall be placed in many trying ones, my reliance will be placed upon you and the people of the United States—and I wish you to remember, now and forever, that it is your business and not mine—that if the union of these states and the liberties of this people shall be lost, it is but little to any one man of fifty-two years of age, but a great deal to the thirty millions of people who inhabit these United States, and to their posterity in all coming time. It is your business to rise up and preserve the Union and liberty for yourselves, and not for me. I desire they shall be constitutionally preserved.
>
> I, as already intimated, am but an accidental instrument, temporary, and to serve but for a limited time, but I appeal to you again, constantly bear in mind that with you, and not with politicians, not with presidents, not with office-seekers, but with you, is the question, "Shall the Union and shall the liberties of this country be preserved to the latest generations?"

As the train paused for a few moments at Little Falls, New York, Lincoln told the crowd he had neither the time nor the strength to make a speech, and then with the wry humor they loved, said, "I have come to see you and allow you to see me [applause], and as this so far regards the

111

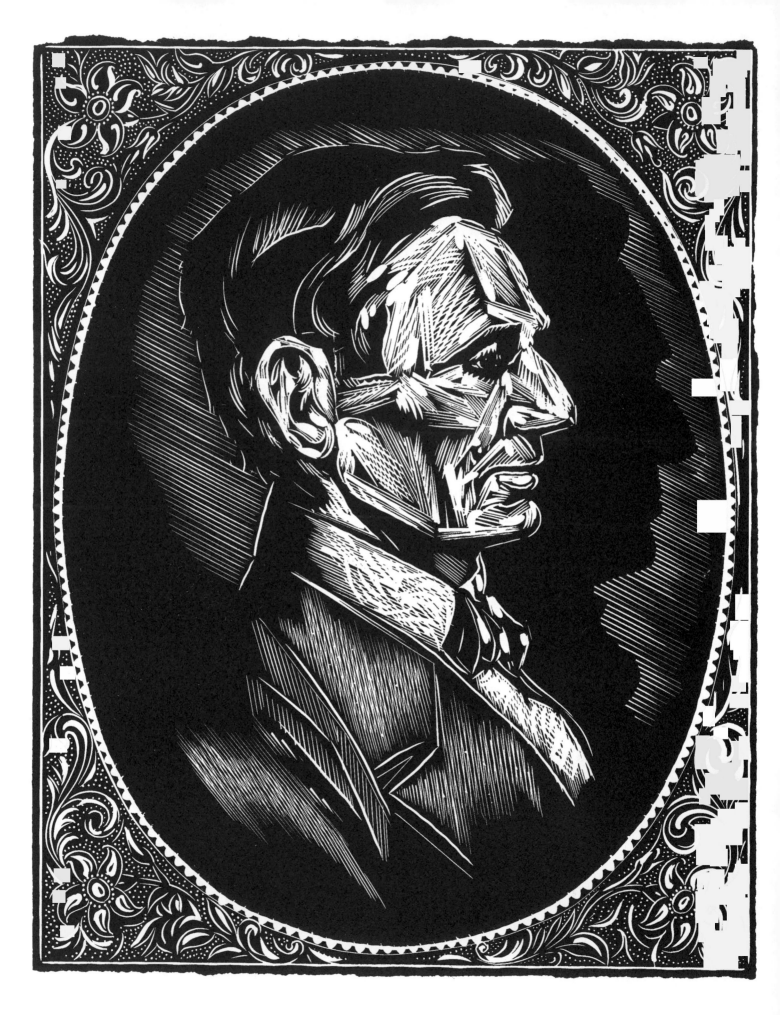

ladies, I have the best of the bargain on my side. I don't make that acknowledgment to the gentlemen [increased laughter], and now I believe I have really made my speech and am ready to bid you farewell when the cars move on."

At Philadelphia, Lincoln came to Independence Hall and in a memorable speech said that the principles upon which he hoped to restore peace to the divided nation sprang from the Declaration of Independence, born in that hallowed place. (The night before, he had been told of a plot to assassinate him on the way through Baltimore.)

I am filled with deep emotion at finding myself standing here in the place where were collected together the wisdom, the patriotism, and devotion to principle, from which sprang the institutions under which we live. You have kindly suggested to me that in my hands is the task of restoring peace to our distracted country. I can say in return that all the political sentiments I entertain have been drawn, so far as I have been able to draw them, from the sentiments which originated and were given to the world from this hall in which we stand. I have never had a feeling politically that did not spring from the sentiments embodied in the Declaration of Independence. I have often pondered over the dangers which were incurred by the men who assembled here and adopted that Declaration of Independence. I have pondered over the toils that were endured by the officers and soldiers of the army, who achieved that Independence. I have often inquired of myself, what great principle or idea it was that kept this confederacy so long together. It was not the mere matter of the separation of the colonies from the motherland but something in that Declaration giving liberty, not alone to the people of this country, but hope to the world for all future time. It was that which gave promise that in due time the weights should be lifted from the shoulders of all men, and that all should have an equal chance. This is the sentiment embodied in that Declaration of Independence.

Now, my friends, can this country be saved upon that basis? If it can, I will consider myself one of the happiest men in the world if I can help to save it. If it can't be saved upon that principle, it will be truly awful. But if this country cannot be saved without giving up that principle, I was about to say I would rather be assassinated on this spot than to surrender it.

Now, in my view of the present aspect of affairs, there is no need of bloodshed and war. There is no necessity for it. I am not in favor of such a course, and I may say in advance, there will be no blood shed unless it be forced upon the government. The government will not use force unless force is used against it.

My friends, this is a wholly unprepared speech. I did not expect to be called upon to say a word when I came here—I supposed I was merely to do something toward raising a flag. I may, therefore, have said something indiscreet, but I have said nothing but what I am willing to live by, and, in the pleasure of Almighty God, die by.

The next day, arriving in Washington, he told a Virginian urging him to accept a compromise with the South:

In a choice of evils, war may not always be the worst. Still I would do all in my power to avert it, except to neglect a constitutional duty. As to slavery, it must be content with what it has. The voice of the civilized world is against it; it is opposed to its growth or extension. Freedom is a natural condition of the human race in which the Almighty intended men to live. Those who fight the purpose of the Almighty will not succeed. They have always been, they will always be, beaten.

10

WE MUST NOT BE ENEMIES

O<small>N MARCH 4, 1861, LINCOLN GAVE</small> his First Inaugural Address. He had worked long and hard on it. Thirty thousand people standing on the East Plaza before the Capitol listened to him in deep silence.

He was trying to hold back the tide of secession. He wanted to preserve the Union in the name of freedom. He wanted to prove to a world dominated by kings and despots that a republic founded on liberty and democracy could endure. He appealed to the South not to destroy this experiment in democratic self-government.

These are some of the key passages from Lincoln's First Inaugural Address:

> It is seventy-two years since the first inauguration of a president under our national Constitution. During that period fifteen different and greatly distinguished citizens have, in succession, administered the executive branch of the government. They have conducted it through many perils and, generally, with great success. Yet, with all this scope for precedent, I now enter upon the same task, for the brief constitutional term of four years, under great and peculiar difficulty. A disruption of the Federal Union, heretofore only menaced, is now formidably attempted.

I hold that in contemplation of universal law and the Constitution, the Union of these states is perpetual. Perpetuity is implied, if not expressed, in the fundamental law of all national governments. It is safe to assert that no government proper ever had a provision in its organic law for its own termination. Continue to execute all the express provisions of our national Constitution, and the Union will endure forever—it being impossible to destroy it, except by some action not provided for in the instrument itself.

Again, if the United States be not a government proper but an association of states in the nature of contract merely, can it, as a contrast, be peaceably unmade by less than all the parties who made it? One party to a contract may violate it—break it, so to speak; but does it not require all to lawfully rescind it?

Descending from these general principles, we find the proposition that, in legal contemplation, the Union is perpetual, confirmed by the history of the Union itself. The Union is much older than the Constitution. It was formed, in fact, by the Articles of Association in 1774. It was matured and continued by the Declaration of Independence in 1776. It was further matured and the faith of all the then thirteen states expressly plighted and engaged that it should be perpetual, by the Articles of Confederation in 1777. And finally, in 1787, one of the declared objects for ordaining and establishing the Constitution was "to form a more perfect union."

But if destruction of the Union by one, or by a part only of the states, be lawfully possible, the Union is less perfect than before the Constitution, having lost the vital element of perpetuity.

Sojourner Truth

It follows from these views that no state, upon its own mere motion, can lawfully get out of the Union—that resolves and ordinances to that effect are legally void and that acts of violence, within any state or states, against the authority of the United States, are insurrectionary or revolutionary, according to circumstances.

I therefore consider that, in view of the Constitution and the laws, the Union is unbroken; and, to the extent of my ability, I shall take care, as the Constitution itself expressly enjoins upon me, that the laws of the Union be faithfully executed in all the states. Doing this I deem to be only a simple duty on my part; and I shall perform it, so far as practicable, unless my rightful masters, the American people, shall withhold the requisite means or in some authoritative manner direct the contrary. I trust this will not be regarded as a menace, but only as the declared purpose of the Union that it will constitutionally defend and maintain itself.

In doing this there need to be no bloodshed or violence; and there shall be none, unless it be forced upon the national authority. The power confided to me will be used to hold, occupy, and possess the property and places belonging to the government, and to collect the duties and imposts; but beyond what may be necessary for these objects, there will be no invasion—no using of force against or among the people anywhere. . . .

That there are persons in one section or another who seek to destroy the Union at all events, and are glad of any pretext to do it, I will neither affirm nor deny; but if there be such, I need address no word to them. To those, however, who really love the Union, may I not speak?

Before entering upon so grave a matter as the destruction of our national fabric, with all its benefits, its memories, and its hopes, would it not be wise to ascertain precisely why we do it? Will you hazard so desperate a step, while there is any possibility that any portion of the ills you fly from have no real existence? Will you, while the certain ills you fly to are greater than all the real ones you fly from? Will you risk the commission of so fearful a mistake?

All profess to be content in the Union, if all constitutional rights can be maintained. Is it true, then, that any right, plainly written in the Constitution, has been denied? I think not. Happily, the human mind is so constituted that no party can reach to the audacity of doing this. Think, if you can, of a single instance in which a plainly written provision of the Constitution has ever been denied. If, by the mere force of numbers, a majority should deprive a minority of any clearly written constitutional right, it might, in a moral point of view, justify revolution—certainly would, if such a right were a vital one. But such is not our case. All the vital rights of minorities and of individuals are so plainly assured to them, by affirmations and negations, guarantees and prohibitions, in the Constitution that controversies never arise concerning them. But no organic law can ever be framed with a provision specifically applicable to every question which may occur in practical administration. No foresight can anticipate, nor any document of reasonable length contain, express provisions for all possible questions. Shall fugitives from labor be surrendered by national or by state authority? The Constitution does not expressly say. May Congress prohibit slavery in the territories? The Constitution does not expressly say. Must

Congress protect slavery in the territories? The Constitution does not expressly say.

From questions of this class spring all our constitutional controversies, and we divide upon them into majorities and minorities. If the minority will not acquiesce, the majority must, or the government must cease. There is no other alternative; for continuing the government is acquiescence on one side or the other. If a minority, in such case, will secede rather than acquiesce, they make precedent which, in turn, will divide and ruin them; for a minority of their own will secede from them, whenever a majority refuses to be controlled by such minority. For instance, why may not any portion of a new confederacy, a year or two hence, arbitrarily secede again, precisely as portions of the present Union now claim to secede from it. All who cherish disunion sentiments are now being educated to the exact temper of doing this. Is there such perfect identity of interests among the states to compose a new Union, as to produce harmony only and prevent renewed secession?

Plainly, the central idea of secession is the essence of anarchy. A majority, held in restraint by constitutional checks and limitations and always changing easily, with deliberate changes of popular opinions and sentiments, is the only true sovereign of a free people. Whoever rejects it, does, of necessity, fly to anarchy or to despotism. Unanimity is impossible; the rule of a minority as a permanent arrangement is wholly inadmissable; so that rejecting the majority principle, anarchy or despotism in some form is all that is left. . . .

One section of our country believes slavery is right and ought to be extended, while the other believes it is wrong and ought not to be extended. This is the only substantial dispute. The fugitive slave clause of the Constitution, and the law for the suppression of the foreign slave trade, are each as well enforced, perhaps, as any law can ever be in a community where the moral sense of the people imperfectly supports the law itself. The great body of the people abide by the dry legal obligation in both cases, and a few break over in each. This, I think, cannot be perfectly cured; and it would be worse in both cases after the separation of the sections than before. The foreign slave trade, now imperfectly suppressed, would be ultimately revived without restriction in one section; while fugitive slaves, now only partially surrendered, would not be surrendered at all by the other.

Physically speaking, we cannot separate. We cannot remove our respective sections from each other nor build an impassable wall between them. A husband and wife may be divorced and go out of the presence and beyond the reach of each other, but the different parts of our country cannot do this. They cannot but remain face-to-face; and intercourse, either amicable or hostile, must continue between them. Is it possible, then, to make that intercourse more advantageous or more satisfactory after separation than before? Can aliens make treaties easier than friends can make laws? Can treaties be more faithfully enforced between aliens than laws can among friends? Suppose you go to war, you cannot fight always; and when, after much loss on both sides and no gain on either, you cease fighting, the identical old questions as to terms of intercourse are again upon you.

This country, with its institutions, belongs to the people who inhabit it. Whenever they shall grow weary of the

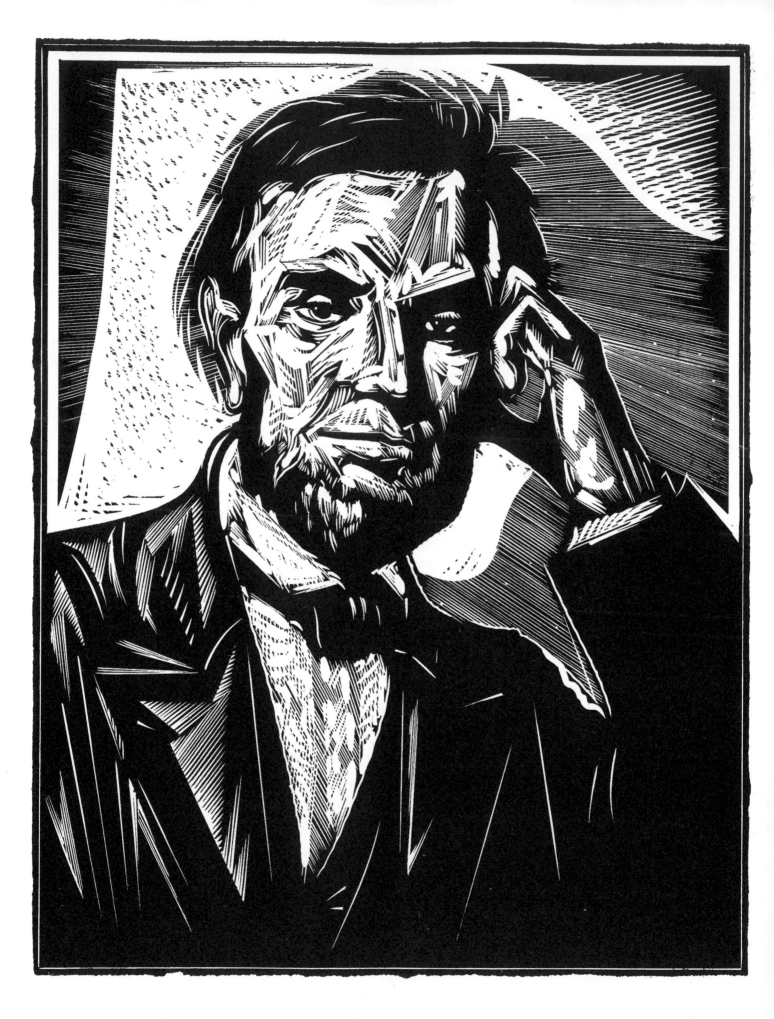

existing government, they can exercise their constitutional right of amending it or their revolutionary right to dismember or overthrow it. I cannot be ignorant of the fact that many worthy and patriotic citizens are desirous of having the national constitution amended. While I make no recommendation of amendments, I fully recognize the rightful authority of the people over the whole subject, to be exercised in either of the modes prescribed in the instrument itself; and I should, under existing circumstances, favor, rather than oppose, a fair opportunity being afforded the people to act upon it. . . .

My countrymen, one and all, think calmly and well upon this whole subject. Nothing valuable can be lost by taking time. If there be an object to hurry any of you, in hot haste, to a step which you would never take deliberately, that object will be frustrated by taking time; but no good object can be frustrated by it. Such of you as are now dissatisfied still have the old Constitution unimpaired, and, on the sensitive point, the laws of your own framing under it; while the new administration will have no immediate power, if it would, to change either. If it were admitted that you who are dissatisfied hold the right side in the dispute, there still is no single good reason for precipitate action. Intelligence, patriotism, Christianity, and a firm reliance on Him who has never yet forsaken this favored land, are still competent to adjust, in the best way, all our present difficulty.

In your hands, my dissatisfied fellow countrymen, and not in mine, is the momentous issue of civil war. The government will not assail you. You can have no conflict without being yourselves the aggressors. You have no oath registered in Heaven to destroy the government, while I shall have the most solemn one to "preserve, protect, and defend" it.

I am loath to close. We are not enemies but friends. We must not be enemies. Though passion may have strained, it must not break our bonds of affection. The mystic chords of memory, stretching from every battlefield and patriot grave to every living heart and hearthstone, all over this broad land, will yet swell the chorus of the Union, when again touched, as surely they will be, by the better angels of our nature.

11

THE
GUNS
ROAR

THE SOUTH DID NOT LISTEN. IN HIS First Inaugural, Lincoln had made perhaps the most eloquent statement of what America meant to the world, but it had no effect upon the seceded states. The Confederates took his determination to hold on to Fort Sumter, at the entrance to the harbor of Charleston, South Carolina, as a provocation.

Just five weeks after Lincoln took office, Confederate guns fired on Fort Sumter, beginning the Civil War. Lincoln called it an "insurrection" and asked for seventy-five thousand men to volunteer for three months to put it down. In a war message to Congress on July 4, 1861, he explained the issues at stake:

> This issue embraces more than the fate of these United States. It presents to the whole family of man the question whether a constitutional republic or a democracy—a government of the people, by the same people—can, or cannot, maintain its territorial integrity against its own domestic foes. It presents the question whether discontented individuals, too few in numbers to control administration, according to organic law, in any case, can always, upon the pretenses made in this case or on any other pretenses, or

arbitrarily without any pretense, break up their government, and thus practically put an end to free government
upon the earth. It forces us to ask: Is there, in all republics,
this inherent, and fatal weakness? Must a government, of
necessity, be too strong for the liberties of its own people
or too weak to maintain its own existence?

So viewing the issue, no choice was left but to call out
the war power of the government; and so to resist force,
employed for its destruction, by force, for its preservation. . . .

This is essentially a people's contest. On the side of
the Union, it is a struggle for maintaining in the world that
form and substance of government whose leading object is
to elevate the condition of men, to lift artificial weights from
all shoulders, to clear the paths of laudable pursuit for all,
to afford all an unfettered start and a fair chance in the
race of life. Yielding to partial and temporary departures
from necessity, this is the leading object of the government
for whose existence we contend. . . .

Our popular government has often been called an experiment. Two points in it our people have already settled:
the successful establishing and the successful administering
of it. One still remains: its successful maintenance against
a formidable internal attempt to overthrow it. It is now for
them to demonstrate to the world that those who can fairly
carry an election, can also suppress a rebellion; that ballots
are the rightful and peaceful successors of bullets; and that
when ballots have fairly and constitutionally decided, there
can be no successful appeal back to bullets; that there can
be no successful appeal, except to ballots themselves, at
succeeding elections. Such will be a great lesson of peace—

William H Carney

teaching men that what they cannot take by an election, neither can they take it by a war—teaching all, the folly of being the beginners of a war.

Few foresaw that this would be a long war, a war that would last four years and bring enormous losses to both sides. It began with the North far stronger than the South. Lincoln could count on the support of twenty-three states with twenty-two million people; a solid structure of industry, agriculture, and finance; a developed railway system; and a good merchant marine. Davis had only eleven states behind him, with nine million people—a third of them slaves. The South was a plantation economy, its industry small, its finances weak, its railroads thinly scattered, its few good harbors easily blockaded. As for resources in fighting men, the North could call up two million, the South only eight hundred thousand.

The war was fought mainly by volunteer soldiers. The generals were mostly West Pointers who had served in the Mexican War and the peace-time army. Their personal jealousies were strong and made Lincoln's work as commander in chief all the more difficult. Both sides were poorly prepared to recruit, equip, train, and maintain the huge forces needed.

In the North, many people opposed using military power to hold the Union together. In the South, some were still loyal to the Union, believing the Confederacy was fighting not for the common good but only to hang on to slavery. That was why the western part of Virginia cut away from the state and joined the Union as the new free state of West Virginia. The border slave states—Maryland, Missouri, and Kentucky—stayed with the Union, and Lincoln did everything possible to keep their loyalty.

Maryland, which bordered the national capital, became Lincoln's special concern when pro-Confederate groups began to arm and drill. He therefore suspended the writ of habeas corpus (guaranteed by the Constitution) in that part of Maryland and sent federal troops to occupy Baltimore and other key points.

This was an early example of Lincoln's very broad interpretation of a president's war powers invoked to meet a great emergency.

In his war message of July 1861, Lincoln gave his reason for suspending the writ of habeas corpus:

> Soon after the first call for militia, it was considered a duty to authorize the Commanding General, in proper cases, according to his discretion, to suspend the privilege of the writ of habeas corpus; or, in other words, to arrest and detain without resort to the ordinary processes and forms of law such individuals as he might deem dangerous to the public safety. This authority has purposely been exercised but very sparingly. Nevertheless, the legality and propriety of what has been done under it are questioned; and the attention of the country has been called to the proposition that one who is sworn to "take care that the laws be faithfully executed" should not himself violate them.

> Of course some consideration was given to the questions of power and propriety before this matter was acted upon. The whole of the laws which were required to be faithfully executed were being resisted and failing of execution in nearly one-third of the states. Must they be allowed to finally fail of execution, even had it been perfectly clear that by the use of the means necessary to their execution, some single law, made in such extreme tenderness of the citizen's liberty that practically it relieves more of the guilty than of the innocent, should, to a very limited extent, be violated?

> To state the question more directly, are all the laws but one to go unexecuted and the government itself to go to pieces lest that one be violated? Even in such a case,

would not the official oath be broken, if the government should be overthrown, when it was believed that disregarding the single law would tend to preserve it? But it was not believed that this question was presented. It was not believed that any law was violated. The provision of the Constitution that "the privilege of the writ of habeas corpus shall not be suspended unless when, in cases of rebellion or invasion, the public safety may require it" is equivalent to a provision—is a provision—that such privilege may be suspended when, in cases of rebellion or invasion, the public safety does require it. It was decided that we have a case of rebellion and that the public safety does require the qualified suspension of the privilege of the writ, which was authorized to be made.

When the opposition called him a tyrant for this, Lincoln replied:

I do not intend to be a tyrant. At all events I shall take care that in my own eyes I do not become one. I have no right to act the tyrant to mere political opponents. If a man votes for supplies of men and money, encourages enlistments, discourages desertions, does all in his power to carry the war on to a successful issue, I have no right to question him for his abstract political opinions. I must make a dividing line somewhere between those who are the opponents of the government, and those who only approve peculiar features of my administration while they sustain the government.

Later, when Lincoln had the army arrest without charge thousands of Northern Democrats—called "Copperheads"—who campaigned against the war and voiced sympathy with the South, their fellow Democrats angrily

protested. In a long public defense of his action, Lincoln made this telling point:

> **Must I shoot a simpleminded soldier boy who deserts, while I must not touch a hair of a wily agitator who induces him to desert? This is none the less injurious when effected by getting a father or brother or friend into a public meeting and there working upon his feelings till he is persuaded to write the soldier boy that he is fighting for a bad cause, for a wicked administration of a contemptible government too weak to arrest and punish him if he shall desert. I think that in such a case to silence the agitator and save the boy is not only constitutional but withal a great mercy.**

The fighting would reach into every slave state but Delaware, and up into five of the Northern states. But the main focus was Virginia, where Richmond, now the Confederate capital, was only one hundred miles south of Washington. The Union meant to capture it, while the South sought to defend it. For two long years the Union suffered a series of defeats on that Virginia front, beginning with the disaster at Bull Run.

Lincoln followed the course of the battles closely, trying to manage the military while giving hours daily to meeting with his Cabinet members, senators, congressmen, office-seekers, and ordinary citizens. To relax he would take carriage rides or go to the theater or to concerts. He wrote many letters, both business and personal. He could be touchingly warm to strangers who tendered him the smallest token of support, as when he wrote to thank a woman "for the gift of a pair of socks so fine and soft and warm [it] could hardly have been manufactured in any other way than the old Kentucky fashion."

The letters Lincoln wrote to his generals offer examples of his mixture of firmness and tact. Many of the officers complained of being neglected, of not having enough supplies or men, of being bypassed in promotions, and so on. Major General David Hunter, appointed military commander of Kansas in November 1861, soon wrote Lincoln, blaming him for not giving him command of a large-enough army. When Lincoln replied, he told his special messenger to hold off on delivering the letter until Hunter was "in a good humor":

> I am constrained to say it is difficult to answer so ugly a letter in good temper. I am, as you intimate, losing much of the great confidence I placed in you, not from any act or omission of yours touching the public service up to the time you were sent to Leavenworth, but from the flood of grumbling dispatches and letters I have seen from you since. I knew you were being ordered to Leavenworth at the time it was done; and I aver that with as tender a regard for your honor and your sensibilities as I had for my own, it never occurred to me that you were being "humiliated, insulted, and disgraced"; nor have I, up to this day, heard an intimation that you have been wronged, coming from anyone but yourself. . . .
>
> I have been, and am sincerely, your friend; and if, as such, I dare to make a suggestion, I would say you are adopting the best possible way to ruin yourself. "Act well your part, there all the honor lies." He who does something at the head of one regiment, will eclipse him who does nothing at the head of a hundred. Your friend as ever . . .

Lincoln expressed his idea of how the war should be fought in a letter to General Don Carlos Buell early in 1862:

> I state my general idea of this war to be that we have the greater numbers, and the enemy has the greater facility of concentrating forces upon points of collision; that we

must fail, unless we can find some way of making our advantage an over-match for his; and that this can only be done by menacing him with superior forces at different points at the same time, so that we can safely attack one, or both, if he makes no change; and if he weakens one to strengthen the other, forbear to attack the strengthened one, but seize and hold the weakened one, gaining so much.

George B. McClellan, whom Lincoln named commanding general early in the war, gave the president all kinds of trouble, including direct insults at times. He never seemed to want to engage the enemy, always demanding more troops to meet Confederate forces whose strength he constantly exaggerated. In February 1862 McClellan said he wanted to ship his army to a place on the Virginia coast from where he would head inland to attack the Confederate capital at Richmond. Lincoln feared the plan would leave Washington unprotected. Instead, he urged McClellan to move straight southward. When he disagreed with McClellan's plans, the president used the simplest way of challenging them, as this message of February 3, 1862, indicates:

You and I have distinct and different plans for a movement of the Army of the Potomac.

If you will give me satisfactory answers to the following questions, I shall gladly yield my plan to yours.

1st. Does not your plan involve a greatly larger expenditure of time and money than mine?

2nd. Wherein is a victory more certain by your plan than mine?

3rd. Wherein is a victory more valuable by your plan than mine?

4th. In fact, would it not be less valuable, in this, that

it would break no great line of the enemy's communications, while mine would?

5th. In case of disaster, would not a safe retreat be more difficult by your plan than by mine?

As Union losses mounted, Lincoln kept after McClellan. In October he wrote him:

You remember my speaking to you of what I called your over-cautiousness. Are you not over-cautious when you assume that you cannot do what the enemy is constantly doing? Should you not claim to be at least his equal in prowess, and act upon the claim?

And ten days later, again to the general:

I have just read your dispatch about sore-tongued and fatigued horses. Will you pardon me for asking what the horses of your army have done since the Battle of Antietam that fatigue anything?

In March of 1862, a Massachusetts congressman brought a delegation from his state to meet Lincoln in the White House. (Among them was the author Nathaniel Hawthorne.) The group gave Lincoln a buggy whip, for which he thanked them in these charming but pointed words:

I thank you for your kindness in presenting me with this truly elegant and highly creditable specimen of the handiwork of the mechanics of your state of Massachusetts, and I beg of you to express my hearty thanks to the donors. It displays a perfection of workmanship which I really wish

I had time to acknowledge in more fitting words, and I might then follow your idea that it is suggestive, for it is evidently expected that a good deal of whipping is to be done. But, as we meet here socially, let us not think only of whipping rebels or of those who seem to think only of whipping Negroes, but of those pleasant days which it is to be hoped are in store for us, when, seated behind a good pair of horses, we can crack our whips and drive through a peaceful, happy, and prosperous land. With this idea, gentlemen, I must leave you for my business duties.

12

FOREVER FREE!

NORTHERN MORALE SANK AS THE Union forces failed to win victories. Lincoln was criticized from the Left for not firing McClellan and for refusing to proclaim emancipation. The editor Horace Greeley published an open letter to Lincoln in his *New York Tribune*, begging the president to turn the war into a crusade for freedom. Lincoln's public reply was a careful balancing of appeals to both conservatives and radicals. While holding that preservation of the Union was the war aim, he hinted that emancipation might come if it was needed to save the Union:

> I would save the Union. I would save it the shortest way under the Constitution. The sooner the national authority can be restored, the nearer the Union will be "the Union as it was." If there be those who would not save the Union unless they could at the same time save slavery, I do not agree with them. If there be those who would not save the Union unless they could at the same time destroy slavery, I do not agree with them. My paramount object in this struggle is to save the Union, and is not either to save or to destroy slavery. If I could save the Union without freeing any slave I would do it; and if I could save it by freeing some and leaving others alone I would also do that. What

I do about slavery and the colored race, I do because I believe it helps to save the Union; and what I forbear, I forbear because I do not believe it would help to save the Union. I shall do less whenever I shall believe what I am doing hurts the cause, and I shall do more whenever I shall believe doing more will help the cause. I shall try to correct errors when shown to be errors; and I shall adopt new views so fast as they shall appear to be true views.

I have here stated my purpose according to my view of official duty; and I intend no modification of my oft-expressed personal wish that all men everywhere could be free.

Actually, Lincoln had already decided to issue the Emancipation Proclamation. He had moved slowly in order to mobilize the greatest number of Northerners behind the war and to avoid antagonizing the border slave states. He knew racism infected the North; few soldiers were ready to die to free the slaves. Yet with each defeat, public feeling shifted. The abolitionists, like Greeley, feared a peace might be reached by a compromise with the Confederacy that would leave slavery untouched. But as the tides of war began to turn in the Union's favor, Lincoln determined he would use the presidential war power as the quickest way to end slavery.

On July 22, 1862, he read his first draft of the Emancipation Proclamation to a cabinet meeting. It ended with the words:

And as a fit and necessary military measure for effecting this object, I, as commander in chief of the Army and Navy of the United States, do order and declare that on the first day of January in the Year of Our Lord one thousand eight hundred and sixty-three, all persons held as slaves within any state or states, wherein the constitutional authority of the United States shall not then be prac-

Frederick Douglass

tically recognized, submitted to, and maintained, shall then, thenceforward and forever, be free.

Cabinet members urged Lincoln to hold back on publishing the proclamation. He agreed to wait for better news from the battlefield so as to avoid its being viewed as a loser's desperate measure. Lincoln's decision transformed the war. Now it was a war to preserve the Union *and* to end slavery. There would be no compromise; it would be fought to the bitter end.

Two months later, on September 22, after the Union's victory at Antietam, Lincoln released the preliminary proclamation. He was warning the South to end the rebellion within a hundred days or face the taking away of their slave property "forever." The press took it as a revolutionary measure, with the antislavery forces praising it and the South damning Lincoln as a "savage."

A month before the proclamation would take effect, Lincoln sent his second annual message to Congress. Using his war powers, he would free the slaves in areas still in rebellion, where he had, as yet, no enforceable authority. Now, to Congress he outlined a plan for gradual emancipation of slaves in the border states loyal to the Union, with compensation to the owners and colonization of the freed people if they consented. Here are the last lines of that message—one of the most moving passages Lincoln ever wrote:

The dogmas of the quiet past are inadequate to the stormy present. The occasion is piled high with difficulty, and we must rise with the occasion. As our case is new, so we must think anew and act anew. We must disenthrall ourselves, and then we shall save our country.

Fellow citizens, we cannot escape history. We of this Congress and this administration will be remembered in spite of ourselves. No personal significance or insignificance can spare one or another of us. The fiery trial through which we pass will light us down, in honor or dishonor, to the latest generation. We say we are for the Union. The world will not forget that we say this. We know how to save the Union. The world knows we do know how to save it. We—even we here—hold the power and bear the responsibility. In giving freedom to the slave, we assure freedom to the free—honorable alike in what we give and what we preserve. We shall nobly save, or meanly lose, the last best hope of earth. Other means may succeed; this could not fail. The way is plain, peaceful, generous, just—a way which, if followed, the world will forever applaud, and God must forever bless.

On January 1, 1863, Lincoln did what he had promised: he issued the final Emancipation Proclamation. Throughout the North and in those parts of the South held by Union troops, crowds cheered as the words "forever free" came over the wires. In Washington, great processions of blacks and whites crowded up to the White House to congratulate the president. He came to the window and bowed to them. To African-Americans emancipation meant the nation now had the chance to live up to the promise of its democratic ideals.

The Emancipation Proclamation was framed in legal language—quite unlike Lincoln's style in most of his statements. Nevertheless, wrote his biographer Stephen B. Oates, it was "the most revolutionary measure ever to come from an American president up to that time." It tore at the roots of the South's social and economic order. As Lincoln's armies captured rebel territory, they freed the slaves. The grip of slavery loosened with every Union victory. Even before federal troops reached them, thousands of slaves "voted with their feet" for freedom.

The proclamation liberated Lincoln himself. It cut the barrier that had separated the private citizen from the public statesman. The institution he had always hated as a humane man he could now destroy by his constitutional power as war president. "If my name ever goes into history," he said, "it will be for this act."

Burdened as he was by the relentless pressure of great decisions, he still gave time to comfort men and women afflicted by war. When a Union officer Lincoln had known back in Illinois was killed in combat, the president wrote this warm letter of sympathy to Colonel McCullough's daughter:

Dear Fanny:

It is with deep grief that I learn of the death of your kind and brave father; and, especially, that it is affecting your young heart beyond what is common in such cases. In this sad world of ours, sorrow comes to all; and, to the young, it comes with bitterest agony because it takes them unawares. The older have learned to ever expect it. I am anxious to afford some alleviation of your present distress. Perfect relief is not possible, except with time. You can not now realize that you will ever feel better. Is not this so? And yet it is a mistake. You are sure to be happy again. To know this, which is certainly true, will make you some less miserable now. I have had experience enough to know what I say; and you need only to believe it, to feel better at once. The memory of your dear father, instead of an agony, will yet be a sad sweet feeling in your heart, of a purer and holier sort than you have known before.

Please present my kind regards to your afflicted mother.

Your sincere friend

After a serious defeat at Fredericksburg, the morale of the Army of the Potomac dropped dangerously. Officers complained that the disgrace of the disaster was due to stupidity and bungling. They began to talk of the need for a dictator to take charge. Lincoln replaced the commanding officer with the popular General Joseph Hooker, but gave him this warning:

> I have heard, in such a way as to believe it, of your recently saying that both the Army and the government needed a dictator. Of course it was not for this, but in spite of it, that I have given you the command. Only those generals who gain successes can set up dictators. What I now ask of you is military success, and I will risk the dictatorship.

In the midsummer of 1863, Charles Halpine, an Irish-born army officer who had won fame as the humorist "Miles O'Reilly," visited the White House. He was dismayed to find a large crowd of people waiting to see Lincoln. When he was admitted, he asked the president why he didn't have these visitors screened in advance, so that only the most important would get in to see him? Lincoln's reply is another proof of his closeness to the people he sprang from:

> I feel—though the tax on my time is heavy—that no hours of my day are better employed than those which thus bring me again within the direct contact and atmosphere of the average of our whole people. Men moving only in an official circle are apt to become merely official—not to say arbitrary—in their ideas, and are apter and apter, with each passing day, to forget that they only hold power in a representative capacity.
>
> Now this is all wrong. I go into these promiscuous receptions of all who claim to have business with me twice each week, and every applicant for audience has to take

his turn, as if waiting to be shaved in a barber's shop. Many of the matters brought to my notice are utterly frivolous, but others are of more or less importance, and all serve to renew in me a clearer and more vivid image of that great popular assemblage out of which I sprung, and to which at the end of two years I must return. I tell you . . . that I call these receptions my "public-opinion bath"; for I have but little time to read the papers and gather public opinion that way; and though they may not be pleasant in all their particulars, the effect, as a whole, is renovating and invigorating to my perceptions of responsibility and duty.

Always sensitive to public opinion, Lincoln knew how widespread racism was in the North. Most believed this to be "a white man's war." They did not want to see blacks in uniform carrying rifles. Yet from the sound of the first gun, African-Americans had volunteered to fight for the Union. As the long war took a terrible toll in human life, however, people began to change their minds.

Frederick Douglass, a runaway slave who had become the most prominent black leader, tried to make the public realize how blind they were to their own best interests. "What on earth is the matter with the American government and people?" he asked. "Do they really covet the world's ridicule as well as their own social and political ruin?" And pressing the president, too, he said, "Ask Mr. Lincoln if this dark and terrible hour of the nation's extremity is a time for consulting a mere vulgar and unnatural prejudice. . . . This is no time to fight with one hand when both are needed. This is no time to fight with only your white hand and allow your black hand to remain tied."

Given the chance by abolitionist generals, blacks joined up eagerly. Early in 1862, a regiment of volunteers in South Carolina formed under General David Hunter, but after three months of service they were disbanded by government order. Another such group, taken into service by

General Jim Lane in Kansas, saw action twice against rebel guerrillas, but it, too, was disbanded.

Finally, after the Emancipation Proclamation, Lincoln opened the Union ranks to blacks. In March 1863, in a letter to Governor Andrew Johnson of Tennessee, he explained why raising black troops was so important:

I am told you have at least thought of raising a Negro military force. In my opinion the country now needs no specific thing so much as some man of your ability and position to go to this work. When I speak of your position, I mean that of an eminent citizen of a slave state, and himself a slaveholder. The colored population is the great available, and yet unavailed of, force for restoring the Union. The bare sight of fifty thousand armed and drilled black soldiers on the banks of the Mississippi would end the rebellion at once. And who doubts that we can present that sight, if we but take hold in earnest? If you have been thinking of it, please do not dismiss the thought.

Lincoln knew how the sight of black soldiers facing them in combat would infuriate the Confederates. He advised General Hunter what to do about it:

I am glad to see the accounts of your colored force at Jacksonville, Florida. I see the enemy are driving at them fiercely, as is to be expected. It is important to the enemy that such a force shall not take shape and grow and thrive in the South; and in precisely the same proportion, it is important to us that it shall. Hence the utmost caution and vigilance is necessary on our part. The enemy will make extra efforts to destroy them; and we should do the same to preserve and increase them.

Many Northerners, too, were appalled to think that blacks were fighting alongside whites. Hearing that a Union rally would be held in Springfield, Illinois, Lincoln prepared a public letter to be read aloud to his hometown folks. In these passages he made a spirited defense of the enlistment of black troops:

> The war has certainly progressed as favorably for us since the issue of the proclamation as before. I know as fully as one can know the opinions of others that some of the commanders of our armies in the field, who have given us our most important successes, believe the emancipation policy and the use of colored troops constitute the heaviest blow yet dealt to the rebellion; and that at least one of those important successes could not have been achieved when it was but for the aid of black soldiers. Among the commanders holding these views are some who have never had any affinity with what is called abolitionism, or with Republican Party politics, but who hold them purely as military opinions. I submit these opinions as being entitled to some weight against the objections, often urged, that emancipation and arming the blacks are unwise as military measures, and were not adopted, as such, in good faith.
>
> You say you will not fight to free Negroes. Some of them seem willing to fight for you; but no matter. Fight you, then, exclusively to save the Union. I issued the proclamation on purpose to aid you in saving the Union. Whenever you shall have conquered all resistance to the Union, if I shall urge you to continue fighting, it will be an apt

time, then, for you to declare you will not fight to free Negroes.

I thought that in your struggle for the Union, to whatever extent the Negroes should cease helping the enemy, to that extent it weakened the enemy in his resistance to you. Do you think differently? I thought that whatever Negroes can be got to do as soldiers leaves just so much less for white soldiers to do in saving the Union. Does it appear otherwise to you? But Negroes, like other people, act upon motives. Why should they do anything for us, if we will do nothing for them? If they stake their lives for us, they must be prompted by the strongest motive—even the promise of freedom. And the promise being made, must be kept. . . .

When final victory is achieved there will be some black men who can remember that with silent tongue and clenched teeth and steady eye and well-poised bayonet they have helped mankind on to this great consummation, while, I fear, there will be some white ones unable to forget that with malignant heart and deceitful speech they have strove to hinder it.

Not long after, in a message to General U. S. Grant, who was commanding the Western fronts, Lincoln said he was glad to hear of efforts to raise black troops in those parts of the Mississippi Valley where the slaves had been freed: "I believe it is a resource which, if vigorously applied now, will soon close the contest. It works doubly, weakening the enemy and strengthening us."

A battle that changed Northern perceptions of black soldiers was the Union's frontal assault on Fort Wagner, a Confederate earthworks defending the entrance to Charleston Harbor. On July 18, 1863, the Fifty-fourth Massachusetts Infantry, a black regiment led by the young white abolitionist Colonel Robert Gould Shaw, fought so gallantly against terrible odds that it was almost wiped out. Now, said one editor, "the manhood of the colored race shines before many eyes that would not see."

Toward the end of 1863, in his annual message to Congress, Lincoln summed up the value of the black troops for a doubting nation:

> Of those who were slaves at the beginning of the rebellion, full one hundred thousand are now in the United States military service, about one-half of which number actually bear arms in the ranks, thus giving the double advantage of taking so much labor from the insurgent cause and supplying the place which otherwise must be filled with so many white men. So far as tested, it is difficult to say they are not as good soldiers as any. No servile insurrection, or tendency to violence or cruelty, has marked the measure of emancipation and arming the blacks. These measures have been much discussed in foreign countries, and contemporary with such discussion the tone of public sentiment there is much improved. At home the same measures have been fully discussed, supported, criticized, and denounced, and the annual elections following are highly encouraging to those whose official duty it is to bear the country through this great trial. Thus we have the new reckoning. The crisis which threatened to divide the friends of the Union is past.

When the ranks of the Union forces were opened to blacks, promises of equal treatment were made by the government. Those promises were not kept. Blacks suffered unequal pay, allowances, and opportunity throughout the war. For African-Americans it was a two-sided fight: against slavery in the South and against discrimination in the North. Nevertheless, they fought hard and well. By war's end 180,000 had served in Lincoln's

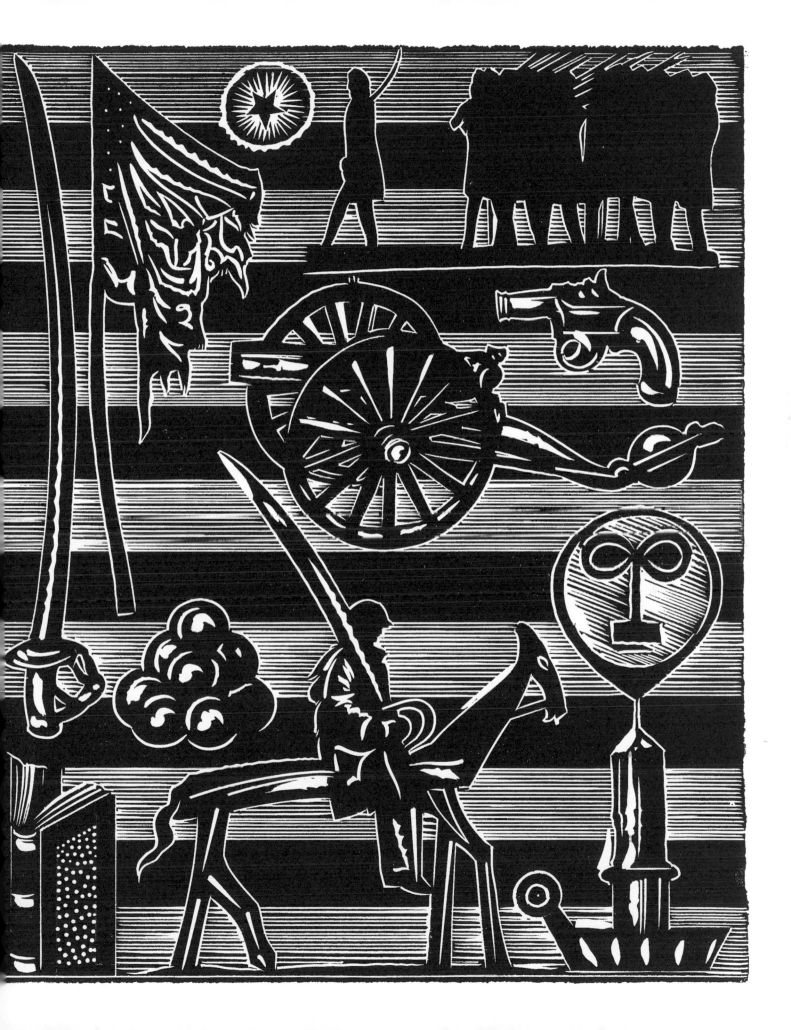

army and 30,000 in the navy, while 250,000 helped the military as laborers. To wipe out slavery 38,000 gave their lives in battle. Twenty-one earned the Congressional Medal of Honor.

In July 1863, the Union won two decisive victories. It turned back a major Confederate drive into the North, defeating Lee's army at Gettysburg, Pennsylvania, on July 4. It was a disaster for the South. It cost the Confederates 28,000 casualties, and the Union, 25,000.

In the West, Grant's troops, after a long siege, finally captured the Confederate city of Vicksburg, Mississippi. When the city fell, 30,000 Confederate soldiers surrendered. The victory gave the Union Army control of the richest plantation region of the South.

Those Union successes were mixed with tragic events on the homefront. In March 1863, Lincoln had put through a draft law to guarantee more manpower. It made all men twenty to forty-five liable for military service. But anyone with three hundred dollars could hire a substitute in his place. That was more money than many workers earned in a whole year. They cried it was a rich man's war and a poor man's fight. They resented the inequality of the law and the expansion of the war aims to include emancipation of the slaves.

Riots broke out in cities across the North—Boston, Albany, Chicago, Cleveland, Detroit. In New York, a week after the July 4 victory at Gettysburg, riots raged in the streets for four days. While homes of the wealthy were looted, the mob's rage turned chiefly against the small free-black population. Blacks were lynched, their homes and shops looted or wrecked, and a black orphanage destroyed. Over one hundred New Yorkers died in the horror.

Conscription created a crisis for Lincoln. He wrote out his arguments for a draft, trying to answer those opposed to it. He read his statement to the cabinet on September 15, but we do not know if he ever gave it as a speech. What he said is still relevant:

The republican institutions and territorial integrity of

our country can not be maintained without the further raising and supporting of armies. There can be no army without men. Men can be had only voluntarily or involuntarily. We have ceased to obtain them voluntarily; and to obtain them involuntarily, is the draft—the conscription. If you dispute the fact and declare that men can still be had voluntarily in sufficient numbers, prove the assertion by yourselves volunteering in such numbers, and I shall gladly give up the draft. Or if not a sufficient number, but any one of you will volunteer, he for his single self will escape all the horrors of the draft and will thereby do only what each one of at least a million of his manly brethren have already done. Their toil and blood have been given as much for you as for themselves. Shall it all be lost rather than you, too, will bear your part?

I do not say that all who would avoid serving in the war are unpatriotic; but I do think every patriot should willingly take his chance under a law made with great care in order to secure entire fairness. This law was considered, discussed, modified, and amended by Congress—at great length and with much labor—and was finally passed by both branches with a near approach to unanimity. At last, it may not be exactly such as any one man out of Congress, or even in Congress, would have made it. It has been said, and I believe truly, that the Constitution itself is not altogether such as any one of its framers would have preferred. It was the joint work of all, and certainly the better that it was so.

The principle of the draft, which simply is involuntary or enforced service, is not new. It has been practiced in all ages of the world. It was well known to the framers of our Constitution as one of the modes of raising armies; at the time, they placed in that instrument the provision that "the Congress shall have power to raise and support armies." It has been used, just before, in establishing our independence; and it was also used under the Constitution in 1812. Wherein is the peculiar hardship now? Shall we shrink from the necessary means to maintain our free government, which our grandfathers employed to establish it and our own fathers have already employed once to maintain it? Are we degenerate? Has the manhood of our race run out?

On November 19, 15,000 people gathered to dedicate the military cemetery at Gettysburg. The principal address was given by Edward Everett, the popular orator, who talked for two hours. Then Lincoln, who had been asked to say just a few words, stood up and read these three brief paragraphs—272 words; it took him two minutes to speak. His Gettysburg Address is one of the finest examples of writing in the English language:

Fourscore and seven years ago, our fathers brought forth on this continent a new nation, conceived in Liberty and dedicated to the proposition that all men are created equal.

Now we are engaged in a great civil war, testing whether that nation, or any nation so conceived and so dedicated, can long endure. We are met on a great battlefield of that war. We have come to dedicate a portion of that field, as a final resting place for those who here gave their lives that that nation might live. It is altogether fitting and proper that we should do this.

But, in a larger sense, we can not dedicate—we can not consecrate—we can not hallow—this ground. The brave men, living and dead, who struggled here have consecrated it far above our poor power to add or detract. The world will little note nor long remember what we say here, but it can never forget what they did here. It is for us the living, rather, to be dedicated here to the unfinished work which they who fought here have thus far so nobly advanced. It is rather for us to be here dedicated to the great task remaining before us—that from these honored dead we take increased devotion to that cause for which they gave the last full measure of devotion—that we here highly resolve that these dead shall not have died in vain—that this nation, under God, shall have a new birth of freedom—and that government of the people, by the people, for the people, shall not perish from the earth.

Lincoln's words have been committed to memory by countless thousands in their school days. But as in other literary masterpieces, the music of the language does more than please the ear. The Gettysburg Address expresses the profound conviction of Lincoln, and all the people for whom he spoke, that the American experiment in democracy must not be allowed to fail.

13

THE STRONGEST BOND OF HUMAN SYMPATHY

After the victories at Gettysburg and Vicksburg, Lincoln's hopes rose. That fall, in the state elections, Republican campaigners spoke proudly of the deeds of heroic black soldiers and of emancipation as a triumph of justice. The results were a ringing endorsement of Lincoln's administration. Soldiers from many states cast absentee ballots, voting over 90 percent for the Republican candidates. It marked an almost miraculous turn of public opinion in the North.

In the last stages of the war, Lincoln would continue to be occupied with the large questions of military strategy and national politics. But there were also special moments that give us insight into the spirit of the man. It might be a personal letter, a telegraphed message, a quick order, remarks in conversation or in a speech. A sampling helps us get behind the mythic figure.

Despite the worries of war, when his wife was away from the White House, he would write her chatty and reassuring letters:

My dear wife:

All as well as usual, and no particular trouble any way. I put the money into the Treasury at five percent, with the privilege of withdrawing it any time upon thirty days' notice. I suppose you are glad to learn this. Tell dear Tad, poor "Nanny Goat" is lost; and Mrs. Cuthbert and I are

in distress about it. The day you left, Nanny was found resting herself and chewing her little cud on the middle of Tad's bed. But now she's gone! The gardener kept complaining that she destroyed the flowers, till it was concluded to bring her down to the White House. This was done, and the second day she had disappeared and has not been heard of since. This is the last we know of poor "Nanny."

The weather continues dry and excessively warm here. Nothing very important occurring.

His delight in the theater gave Lincoln some relief. From the presidential box one evening he enjoyed James Hackett in his celebrated role as Falstaff. Soon after, the actor sent him a copy of his new book discussing certain plays and actors of Shakespeare. Lincoln replied with this thank-you note:

For one of my age, I have seen very little of the drama. The first presentation of Falstaff I ever saw was yours here, last winter or spring. Perhaps the best compliment I can pay is to say, as I truly can, I am very anxious to see it again. Some of Shakespeare's plays I have never read; while others I have gone over perhaps as frequently as any unprofessional reader. Among the latter are Lear, Richard Third, Henry Eighth, Hamlet, and especially Macbeth. I think nothing equals Macbeth. It is wonderful. Unlike you gentlemen of the profession, I think the soliloquy in Hamlet commencing "O, my offence is rank" surpasses that commencing "To be, or not to be." But pardon this small attempt at criticism. I should like to hear you pronounce the opening speech of Richard the Third. Will you not soon visit Washington again? If you do, please call and let me make your personal acquaintance.

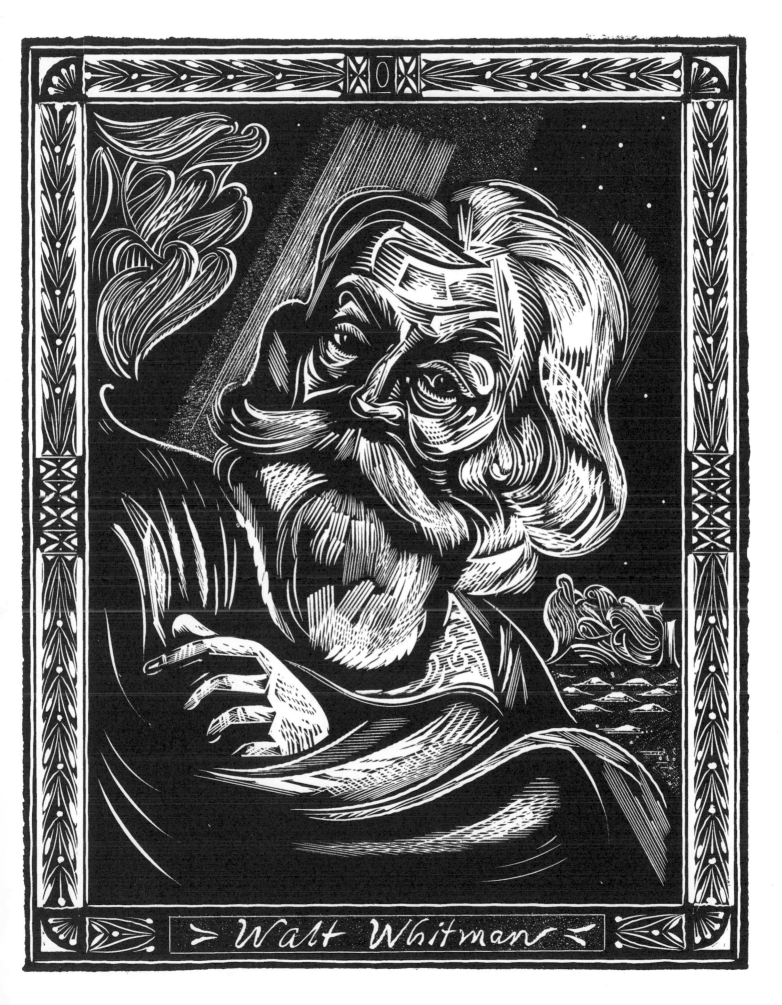

Walt Whitman

Lincoln invited Hackett to the White House and went several times to see his Falstaff. He favored, too, the acting of Edwin Booth as Hamlet and Edwin Forrest as King Lear. He liked to corner a visitor and to read aloud some of his favorite lines from Shakespeare. The power and beauty of the language and the depth of Shakespeare's thought seemed to become part of his innermost self.

Never a drinker, Lincoln was, of course, aware of how common drunkenness was among the people. When the Sons of Temperance came to seek his support, he told them he had always been on their side, and added:

> I think that the reasonable men of the world have long since agreed that intemperance is one of the greatest, if not the very greatest, of all evils amongst mankind. That is not a matter of dispute, I believe. That the disease exists, and that it is a very great one, is agreed upon by all.
>
> The mode of cure is one about which there may be differences of opinion. You have suggested that in an army—our army—drunkenness is a great evil and one which, while it exists to a very great extent, we cannot expect to overcome so entirely as to have such successes in our arms as we might have without it. This undoubtedly is true, and while it is, perhaps, rather a bad source to derive comfort from, nevertheless, in a hard struggle, I do not know but what it is some consolation to be aware that there is some intemperance on the other side, too, and that they have no right to beat us in physical combat on that ground.

To another delegation, this time of working men from New York who wanted to make the president an honorary member of their organization, Lincoln replied:

None are so deeply interested to resist the present rebellion as the working people. Let them beware of prejudice, working division and hostility among themselves. The most notable feature of a disturbance in your city last summer [the New York City draft riots] was the hanging of some working people by other working people. It should never be so. The strongest bond of human sympathy, outside of the family relation, should be one uniting all working people, of all nations and tongues and kindreds. Nor should this lead to a war upon property or the owners of property. Property is the fruit of labor—property is desirable—is a positive good in the world. That some should be rich, shows that others may become rich, and hence is just encouragement to industry and enterprise. Let not him who is houseless pull down the house of another; but let him labor diligently and build one for himself, thus by example assuring that his own shall be safe from violence when built.

Lincoln rarely left Washington, but he did drop in on a war charity fair in Baltimore. (This was the city where people had threatened to lynch him on the way to his inaugural three years before.) In his brief remarks he took up the meaning of the word liberty:

The world has never had a good definition of the word liberty, and the American people, just now, are much in want of one. We all declare for liberty; but in using the same word we do not all mean the same thing. With some the word liberty may mean for each man to do as he pleases with himself and the product of his labor; while with others the same word may mean for some men to do as they please with other men and the product of other men's labor. Here are two not only different but incompatible things, called

175

by the same name—liberty. And it follows that each of the things is, by the respective parties, called by two different and incompatible names—liberty and tyranny.

The shepherd drives the wolf from the sheep's throat, for which the sheep thanks the shepherd as a liberator, while the wolf denounces him for the same act as the destroyer of liberty, especially as the sheep was a black one. Plainly the sheep and the wolf are not agreed upon a definition of the word liberty; and precisely the same difference prevails today among us human creatures, even in the North, and all professing to love liberty. Hence we behold the processes by which thousands are daily passing from under the yoke of bondage, hailed by some as the advance of liberty and bewailed by others as the destruction of all liberty. Recently, as it seems, the people of Maryland have been doing something to define liberty; and thanks to them that, in what they have done, the wolf's dictionary has been repudiated.

Evidence of Lincoln's humane nature can be seen in these brief messages he sent to his generals or to his secretary of war, Edwin Stanton, when he received appeals to lessen harsh punishment of soldiers for desertion (widespread in both the Union and Confederate armies). He took into account specific circumstances:

To General George G. Meade—
At this late moment I am appealed to in behalf of William Thompson of Co. K. 3rd. Maryland Volunteers in 12th Army Corps said to be at Kelly's Ford, under sentence to be shot today as a deserter. He is represented to me to be very young, with symptoms of insanity. Please postpone the execution till further order.

To Edwin M. Stanton—

This woman says her husband and two sons are in the war; that the youngest son, W. J. Klaproth, a private in Co. D, of 143rd. Pennsylvania, volunteers, was wounded, made a prisoner, and paroled at Gettysburg, and is now at Center Street hospital, New Jersey; and that he was under eighteen when he entered the service without the consent of his father or herself. She says she is destitute, and she asks that he may be discharged. If she makes satisfactory proof of the above let it be done.

To Edwin M. Stanton—

This lady says her husband, Theophilus Brown, and his brother, George E. Brown, are in the Old Capitol Prison as prisoners of war, that they were conscripted into the rebel army and were never for the rebel cause and are now willing to do anything reasonable to be at liberty. This may be true, and if true they should be liberated. Please take hold of this case, and do what may seem proper in it.

To General George C. Meade—

I am appealed to in behalf of John Murphy, to be shot tomorrow. His mother says he is but seventeen. Please answer.

To General Stephen A. Hurlbut—

I understand you have under sentence of death a tall old man by the name of Henry F. Luckett. I personally knew him and did not think him a bad man. Please do not let him be executed, unless upon further order from me, and in the meantime send me a transcript of the record.

In another instance, sent the "very bad" record of a soldier named Henry Andrews, Lincoln wrote across it that he had commuted his death sentence to punishment at hard labor for the duration of the war. He added that he did this "not on any merit in the case, but because I am trying to evade the butchering business lately." This was a sign of how crushing was the burden of thousands and thousands of soldiers slaughtered in the war, which at this point had more than another year to run.

And finally, in this note to Stanton, Lincoln recognizes what punishment does, not only to the soldier, but to his family back home:

> A poor widow, by the name of Baird, has a son in the army, that for some offense has been sentenced to serve a long time without pay, or at most, with very little pay. I do not like this punishment of withholding pay—it falls so very hard upon poor families. After he has been serving in this way for several months, at the tearful appeal of the poor mother, I made a direction that he be allowed to enlist for a new term, on the same conditions as others. She now comes and says she can not get it acted upon. Please do it.

When Congress passed the draft law, it made no provision for conscientious objectors. After the Quakers and other pacifist groups protested, Congress voted America's first alternative service law. Conscientious objectors could perform hospital work or care for freedmen as a substitute for military service, or pay a fee of three hundred dollars. But no allowances were made for the refusal of absolute pacifists to cooperate in any way. Lincoln understood that the Quakers were in a "hard dilemma," for while they abhorred war, they also abhorred slavery. He knew they opposed this war as a wrong means to an end they supported and not out of hidden sympathy for the enemy's cause. To Eliza P. Gurney, a prominent Quaker, Lincoln wrote a sympathetic letter, which said, in part:

Your people—the Friends—have had, and are having, a very great trial. On principle and faith, opposed to both war and oppression, they can only practically oppose oppression by war. In this hard dilemma, some have chosen one horn and some the other. For those appealing to me on conscientious grounds, I have done, and shall do, the best I could and can, in my own conscience, under my oath to the law. That you believe this I doubt not; and believing it, I shall still receive, for our country and myself, your earnest prayers to our Father in Heaven.

To delegates from the Baptist Home Mission Society presenting him with resolutions supporting his stand on Emancipation, Lincoln replied with these remarks on Christianity and slavery:

I can only thank you for adding to the effective and almost unanimous support which the Christian communities are so zealously giving to the country, and to liberty. Indeed it is difficult to conceive how it could be otherwise with anyone professing Christianity, or even having ordinary perceptions of right and wrong. To read in the Bible, as the word of God himself, that "in the sweat of thy face shalt thou eat bread," and to preach therefrom that "in the sweat of other men's faces shalt thou eat bread," to my mind can scarcely be reconciled with honest sincerity. When brought to my final reckoning, may I have to answer for robbing no man of his goods; yet more tolerable even this, than for robbing one of himself, and all that was his.

When, a year or two ago, those professedly holy men of the South met in the semblance of prayer and devotion, and, in the name of Him who said, "As ye would all men

should do unto you, do ye even so unto them," appealed to the Christian world to aid them in doing to a whole race of men, as they would have no man do unto themselves, to my thinking, they condemned and insulted God and His church far more than did Satan when he tempted the Savior with the kingdom of the earth. The devil's attempt was no more false and far less hypocritical. But let me forbear, remembering it is also written, "Judge not, lest ye be judged."

A little later, a woman from Tennessee came to the White House to ask Lincoln to release her husband, held as a prisoner of war, because he was a religious man. Lincoln did as she asked, and then said to her:

You say your husband is a religious man; tell him when you meet him, that I say I am not much of a judge of religion, but that, in my opinion, the religion that sets men to rebel and fight against their government, because, as they think, that government does not sufficiently help some men to eat their bread on the sweat of other men's faces, is not the sort of religion upon which people can get to Heaven!

As an Ohio regiment prepared to go home after completing their military service, Lincoln made this brief but emotional farewell to them:

I suppose you are going home to see your families and friends. For the service you have done in this great struggle in which we are engaged I present you sincere thanks for myself and the country. I almost always feel inclined, when I happen to say anything to soldiers, to impress upon them in a few brief remarks the importance of success in this contest. It is not merely for today, but for all time to come, that we should perpetuate for our children's children this great and free government, which we have enjoyed all our lives. I beg you to remember this, not merely for my sake, but for yours.

I happen temporarily to occupy this big White House. I am a living witness that any one of your children may look to come here as my father's child has. It is in order that each of you may have, through this free government which we have enjoyed, an open field and a fair chance for your industry, enterprise, and intelligence; that you may all have equal privileges in the race of life, with all its desirable human aspirations. It is for this the struggle should be maintained, that we may not lose our birthright—not only for one, but for two or three years. The nation is worth fighting for, to secure such an inestimable jewel.

Early in 1864 the reelection of Lincoln was by no means certain. A tradition of one term in the White House was strong. No president had won a second term since Andrew Jackson in 1832. And no president had been renominated by his party since 1840. Besides, several prominent Republicans were pushing themselves for nomination in the belief that they could do as well or better than Lincoln.

Lincoln did not stand idly by waiting for the outcome. He had used patronage to build political support in the North. When the Republicans met in their Baltimore convention in June, they nominated him for president and Andrew Johnson of Tennessee for vice president. The platform backed Lincoln's war measures, called for unconditional surrender of the Confederacy, and endorsed a constitutional amendment to abolish slavery. The Democrats nominated George McClellan on a peace platform.

But politics would have less to do with the election's outcome than winning the war would. The Confederates, now on the defensive, hoped that by hanging on long enough to inflict heavy losses on Lincoln's army, the war-weary North would call it quits without gaining victory.

The Republicans charged the Democrats with "treason" and the Democrats countered by calling Lincoln a "tyrant." Some of their newspapers went so far as to say he was "an imbecile . . . brutal in all his habits . . . filthy . . . obscene . . . an animal."

Nasty names did not cost Lincoln many votes. He was reelected by a majority of 212 to 21 in the electoral college. He won 55 percent of the popular vote, much better than the 48 percent he got from the same states four years earlier. His party swept to victory in the Congress, too.

The very fact of holding an election in the midst of war—and a civil war at that—was itself extraordinary. In no other country before World War II was a general election held during a war. The result of this one would determine the nation's future. Yet as Lincoln explained, "We cannot have free government without elections, and if the rebellion could force us to forego or postpone a national election, it might fairly claim to have already conquered and ruined us."

In March 1864 Lincoln had made Grant supreme commander of the Union armies. Together with General William T. Sherman and General Philip Sheridan, he inflicted terrible losses on the enemy. Their aggressive campaigns chopped up Lee's troops, causing the surrender of Atlanta, Petersburg, and Richmond.

By early 1865 the Confederacy had fallen apart. Union armies occupied many important sections of the South, and the devastation of the crops spread hunger everywhere. Riots and demonstrations against the Confederate government broke out in Southern cities. Rebel army morale collapsed and mass desertions left Lee's generals with only one-third of their manpower.

14

WITH MALICE TOWARD NONE

Long before the war neared its
end, Lincoln and the Congress had begun to think about the complex issue
of how to reconstruct the conquered Southern states. No state had ever
seceded before 1860, so there was no precedent to look back to. The
Constitution said nothing about secession. Facing a new crisis, the president and the Congress each tried to develop programs based upon their
political goals and desires.

Lincoln believed that it was the duty of the president, not the Congress, to restore loyal civilian rule in the South. And he thought the army
the best means to carry it out swiftly. As the Union forces liberated parts
of the South, he pressed army leaders to carry out his reconstruction plans.
His generals helped Southerners who had opposed secession and war to
set up state governments loyal to the Union and pledged to free the slaves.

In Lincoln's desire to restore the seceded states easily and rapidly,
he set terms that the abolitionists, the Radical Republicans, and the black
leaders feared were far too generous. He failed to address the needs of
the four million liberated slaves. They looked to sustained federal power
to aid them in getting a start on an independent economic and political
life and to protect them from their former masters. But Lincoln's policy,
as it was shaped up to his death, would have put the free people back
under the dominion of the whites who controlled the local and state governments. (And that is what did happen, eventually.) The important dif-

ference is that the Thirteenth, Fourteenth, and Fifteenth amendments to the Constitution carried at least the promise of a better future. The Thirteenth Amendment, outlawing slavery, was adopted by Congress on February 1, 1865. Lincoln, though not legally required to, signed the document that would finally put an end to what he had fought against for so long. The other two amendments, adopted after his death, made blacks citizens and gave black men the vote.

The generous nature behind Lincoln's reconstruction proposals is reflected in his Second Inaugural Address. On March 4, 1865, he stood on the platform built at the east front of the Capitol, and as the sun broke through the clouds, he read in ringing tones a short speech that probed the meaning of the long war. Many think this the greatest of all his speeches. The last paragraph has lingered in the memory of generations of Americans:

Fellow Countrymen:

At this second appearing to take the oath of the presidential office, there is less occasion for an extended address than there was at the first. Then a statement, somewhat in detail, of a course to be pursued, seemed fitting and proper. Now, at the expiration of four years, during which public declarations have been constantly called forth on every point and phase of the great contest which still absorbs the attention and engrosses the energies of the nation, little that is new could be presented. The progress of our arms, upon which all else chiefly depends, is as well known to the public as to myself; and it is, I trust, reasonably satisfactory and encouraging to all. With high hope for the future, no prediction in regard to it is ventured.

On the occasion corresponding to this four years ago, all thoughts were anxiously directed to an impending civil war. All dreaded it—all sought to avert it. While the inaugu-

> Ulysses S. Grant <

ral address was being delivered from this place, devoted altogether to saving the Union without war, insurgent agents were in the city seeking to destroy it without war—seeking to dissolve the Union and divide effects by negotiation. Both parties deprecated war, but one of them would make war rather than let the nation survive; and the other would accept war rather than let it perish. And the war came.

One-eighth of the whole population were colored slaves, not distributed generally over the Union, but localized in the Southern part of it. These slaves constituted a peculiar and powerful interest. All knew that this interest was, somehow, the cause of the war. To strengthen, perpetuate, and extend this interest was the object for which the insurgents would rend the Union, even by war; while the government claimed no right to do more than to restrict the territorial enlargement of it. Neither party expected for the war the magnitude or the duration which it has already attained. Neither anticipated that the cause of the conflict might cease with, or even before, the conflict itself should cease. Each looked for an easier triumph and a result less fundamental and astounding. Both read the same Bible and pray to the same God; and each invokes His aid against the other. It may seem strange that any men should dare to ask a just God's assistance in wringing their bread from the sweat of other men's faces; but let us judge not that we be not judged. The prayers of both could not be answered; that of neither has been answered fully. The Almighty has His own purposes. "Woe unto the world because of offenses! For it must needs be that offenses come. But woe to that man by whom the offense cometh!" If we shall suppose that American slavery is one of those offenses

which, in the providence of God, must needs come, but which, having continued through His appointed time, He now wills to remove, and that He gives to both North and South this terrible war, as the woe due to those by whom the offense came, shall we discern therein any departure from those divine attributes which the believers in a Living God always ascribe to Him?

Fondly do we hope—fervently do we pray—that this mighty scourge of war may speedily pass away. Yet, if God wills that it continue until all the wealth piled by the bond-man's two hundred and fifty years of unrequited toil shall be sunk, and until every drop of blood drawn with the lash shall be paid by another drawn with the sword, as was said three thousand years ago, so still it must be said "the judgments of the Lord are true and righteous altogether."

With malice toward none, with charity for all, with firmness in the right, as God gives us to see the right, let us strive on to finish the work we are in; to bind up the nation's wounds, to care for him who shall have borne the battle, and for his widow, and his orphan; to do all which may achieve and cherish a just and a lasting peace, among ourselves and with all nations.

A few weeks later, on April 9, General Lee surrendered to General Grant at Appomattox Courthouse in Virginia. As the Confederate soldiers started for home, Grant told his troops not to cheer, because, he said, "The rebels are our countrymen again." The Confederate government simply evaporated.

The next day the official news of surrender turned Washington into a joyous madhouse. Guns roared, bells rang, flags flew everywhere; men, women, and children crowded the streets, laughing and cheering. In the afternoon, three thousand people followed a brass band to the White House, where they shouted for Lincoln to speak to them. The president came out with his son Tad, waved happily to the crowd, and spoke these words:

Fellow Citizens:

I am very greatly rejoiced to find that an occasion has occurred so pleasurable that the people cannot restrain themselves. [Cheers.] I suppose that arrangements are being made for some sort of a formal demonstration, this, or perhaps, tomorrow night. [Cries of "We can't wait," "We want it now," etc.] If there should be such a demonstration, I, of course, will be called upon to respond, and I shall have nothing to say if you dribble it all out of me before. [Laughter and applause.] I see you have a band of music with you. [Voices: "We have two or three."] I propose closing up this interview by the band performing a particular tune, which I will name. Before this is done, however, I wish to mention one or two little circumstances connected with it. I have always thought "Dixie" one of the best tunes I have ever heard. Our adversaries over the way attempted to appropriate it, but I insisted yesterday that we fairly captured it. [Applause.] I presented the question to the attorney general, and he gave it as his legal opinion that it is our lawful prize. [Laughter and applause.] I now request the band to favor me with its performance.

As an encore, the band struck up "Yankee Doodle."
Four days later, Lincoln was dead.
On April 14—Good Friday—the president and his wife went to see a comedy at Ford's Theater. Waiting for his appearance was John Wilkes Booth, a young Shakespearean actor. He was devoted to the Confederate

cause, believed slavery was good, blamed Lincoln for the war, and hated him intensely. He had gathered together a small band of conspirators in a plot to murder the president and save America from a Yankee dictatorship.

During the performance of the play, Booth managed to slip into the presidential box and shoot Lincoln. The president never regained consciousness, and died the next morning, April 15, 1865. He was fifty-six years old.

A long funeral train carried Lincoln sixteen hundred miles across the country, passing hundreds of thousands of mourners, black and white, to rest at last in the tomb at Springfield.

We cannot know the man in all his dimensions. But in reading what he wrote we can at least hear his own voice.

Brief Profiles of
Lincoln's Contemporaries

Thomas Jefferson
(1743–1826)

Lincoln was born just a few weeks after President Jefferson finished his second term in the White House. Jefferson died on July 4, 1826—the 50th anniversary of his Declaration of Independence. Lincoln, then seventeen, was already an avid reader and a student of young America's history. He cherished the declaration that all men are created with an equal and unalienable right to life, liberty, and the pursuit of happiness as the ideal on which the United States of America was founded. He knew the ideal was not a reality in Jefferson's time nor in his own time, but he believed it was the duty of Americans to bring their institutions closer to that truth. As Lincoln developed his ideas about the unending struggle for freedom and equality, he often cited the rights so eloquently expressed in Jefferson's grandest achievement, the Declaration of Independence.

William Lloyd Garrison
(1805–1879)

William Lloyd Garrison was the best known of the white abolitionists. Born to poverty in Massachusetts, Garrison found work as a newspaperman on local papers and then on abolitionist journals. He founded his own weekly journal, *The Liberator*, in 1831, and soon helped form both New England and American antislavery societies. He called for immediate emancipation and demanded that all churches, political parties, and even the federal government sever ties with the South for its immoral and unchristian labor system. In his speeches and writings, he attacked slavery and slaveholders with powerful language. Many people in the South hated him and placed a price on his head. At the center of the abolitionist crusade for decades, Garrison lived to see slavery destroyed and to be honored for his part in bringing slavery to an end.

Lydia Maria Child
(1802–1880)

Lydia Maria Child, born in Massachusetts, is of great importance for her role in the struggle for black emancipation and equality and for women's rights. Like Lincoln, she believed in the natural rights of all people and the wisdom of the "common man." A schoolteacher in her teens, she soon after became devoted to the movement to abolish slavery and eliminate racism. She wrote tales for children, advice books for wives and mothers, biographies of heroic women, and accounts of the African-American struggle for freedom, as well as novels, stories, and poetry. She wrote a syndicated column on life in New York and for two years edited the *National Anti-Slavery Standard*. Her analysis of race and slavery in *An Appeal in Favor of That Class of Americans Called Africans* (1833) brought many notable Americans into the abolition movement and helped shape the climate of opinion in which Lincoln governed.

HENRY DAVID THOREAU
(1817–1862)

Like Lincoln, Henry David Thoreau is esteemed as one of the greatest American writers. He is known best for his masterwork, *Walden* (1854), the story of his two-year adventure living in a cabin at Walden Pond in Concord, Massachusetts. But he is also remembered for the time in 1846 when he was jailed for refusing to pay his poll tax—an act of protest against the country's unjust war against Mexico, a war he believed was started on behalf of slaveholders who wished to extend their slave territory. Out of that experience came a lecture and an article on civil disobedience, which greatly influenced such leaders as Gandhi and Martin Luther King, Jr. Thoreau, whose family sheltered fugitive slaves, came to the defense of John Brown when the abolitionist was captured at Harpers Ferry and sentenced to be hanged. Thoreau died of tuberculosis, not knowing whether the war to end slavery would succeed.

HARRIET BEECHER STOWE
(1811–1895)

Harriet Beecher Stowe was part of a large Connecticut family headed by Lyman Beecher, a minister known nationally for his leadership of the revivalist movement, who preached about the evil of slavery and the sufferings of the slave. The mother of six children, Stowe wrote sketches to add to the family income. Aroused by the passage of the Fugitive Slave Act of 1850, she began to write scenes of slave life, basing them on simple documentary sources and publishing the chapters serially in an abolitionist paper. In 1852 her story *Uncle Tom's Cabin* was published in book form, and it was as if a torch had been put to a smoldering national issue. From that time on, millions of Americans were made aware of the human anguish of slavery. The public appetite for her book appeared boundless. Readers were challenged to confront slavery's existence as a moral issue. By the time the Civil War broke out, sales ran into the millions. As time went on, inaccurate dramatizations of the novel debased some of the black characters, especially Tom, into racial stereotypes.

ROGER B. TANEY
(1777–1864)

Roger B. Taney had practiced law in Maryland until President Andrew Jackson brought him to Washington. Taney, a Democrat, had been appointed Chief Justice by President Jackson in 1835, after first serving in the President's cabinet as attorney general. One of the most fateful decisions the U.S. Supreme Court ever made was in the Dred Scott case of 1857. Written by Chief Justice Roger B. Taney, it declared that Congress had no power to abolish or prevent slavery in any of the territories, thus making the Missouri Compromise and the Compromise of 1850 unconstitutional. Taney even added that black persons "had no rights which the white man was bound to respect." The decision went far toward nationalizing slavery and was a major factor in bringing on the Civil War.

STEPHEN A. DOUGLAS
(1813–1861)

Stephen A. Douglas, a Vermonter, moved to Illinois, where he taught school and then practiced law. He held several offices before becoming a judge of the state supreme court, then moving on to serve two terms in Congress, where he was a vigorous supporter of the war against Mexico. Elected to the U.S. Senate in 1847, Douglas backed bills permitting territorial governments the freedom to enact laws concerning slavery. That principle of "popular sovereignty" was embedded in his Kansas-Nebraska Bill (1854) and intensified the sectional conflict. It was during the Illinois campaign for the Senate in 1858 that he faced his opponent Lincoln in the famous joint debates over the issue of slavery and its impact on politics, law, and government. While Lincoln emerged as a national figure, Douglas alienated Southern Democrats with his belief that the people of a territory could exclude slavery prior to the formation of a state constitution. As a result, when Douglas won the Democratic nomination for the presidency in 1860, the Southern faction withdrew support from him and ran John C. Breckinridge as their candidate, opening the door for Lincoln—a third-party candidate—to win. When the Civil War began, Douglas gave full support to Lincoln's measures to save the Union.

John Brown
(1800–1859)

Believing that American slavery would not die peacefully, John Brown became the strongest advocate of its militant overthrow. He was born in Connecticut and grew up in Ohio. In the mid-1850s when the troubles in Kansas broke out, Brown and five of his sons went to the territory to help win it for the free-soil movement. He headed a party of eight, who killed five unarmed pro-slavery men at Pottawatomie Creek. The incident roused a great furor and thrust him into the national limelight. Then, in the fall of 1859, with twenty-one followers, Brown struck directly at slavery in the South, seizing the federal arsenal at Harpers Ferry. In the assault, ten of his men were killed and seven captured. Tried for murder and treason, he was hanged on December 2, 1859. Some hailed him as martyr, others condemned him. The stirring "John Brown's Song" sung by Union soldiers on the march kept his name alive.

JEFFERSON DAVIS
(1808–1881)

Jefferson Davis, president of the Confederacy, was born to a small slaveholding family in Kentucky. He went to West Point and became an officer in the same Black Hawk War that Lincoln served in. He also fought in the war with Mexico, winning military fame for heroic action. Owning more than 100 slaves, his devotion to the Southern slave interests dominated his service in the U.S. Senate. Davis resigned in January 1861 when his state seceded from the Union, and soon after he was chosen to head the slave states in rebellion. His rigid personality, autocratic methods, and interference in military matters made him many enemies in the Confederacy. When the South lost the war, he was captured and indicted for treason, but the trial was dropped.

SOJOURNER TRUTH
(1797–1883)

Sojourner Truth (named Isabella at her birth) was born a slave and worked on family farms in New York. Tall, strong, and a hard worker, she was nevertheless beaten by masters and forced into a marriage with a fellow slave. She ran away to freedom in 1826, taking her infant daughter with her, and worked as a domestic servant in New York City for many years. When she became a religious mystic, she took the name of Sojourner Truth and moved about preaching against sin. She was a commanding influence when she spoke at antislavery and women's rights meetings, and her witty and biting arguments for equal rights were often quoted in the press. She taught freedwomen in Washington, D.C., and helped them to find jobs. In her last years she campaigned for the allotment of public lands in the West for African-Americans to settle on.

WILLIAM H. CARNEY
(1840–1904?)

William H. Carney, an African-American, won the Congressional Medal of Honor for his bravery under fire. He had volunteered for the 54th Massachusetts, the infantry regiment that would win lasting fame in the storming of Fort Wagner. As soon as the war began, abolitionists insisted that the Union cause would not triumph unless the war was fought to end slavery. But not until Lincoln issued the Emancipation Proclamation were the Union ranks opened to blacks. Suffering unequal treatment in pay, allowances, and opportunities, black soldiers had to fight a double battle—against slavery in the South and discrimination in the North. The 54th met their first major battle test when they headed the assault on Fort Wagner, a Confederate stronghold. Sergeant Carney, flagbearer for the 54th, said later: "We were fighting for all black men and could not fail." Outnumbered and outgunned, they were ordered back after two desperate bayonet assaults and heavy losses. But they proved their courage and their soldiership. Before the war ended, 210,000 blacks had served in Lincoln's military and 38,000 lost their lives in the battle to end slavery.

FREDERICK DOUGLASS
(1818–1895)

At seventeen, Frederick Douglass declared his independent spirit by fighting his Maryland slavemaster for trying to flog him. Though born a slave, he learned early to read and write and was working in a Baltimore shipyard when he fled north to freedom. Douglass read abolitionist literature and attended their meetings. In 1841 he made a stirring spontaneous speech at the Massachusetts Anti-Slavery Society and was hired as one of its agents. His powerful oratory and his editorship of his own paper, the

North Star, made him the foremost black figure in the abolitionist crusade, and his autobiography became a best-seller overnight. Douglass welcomed the coming of the Civil War, certain it would end slavery, and recruited blacks for the Union forces, including two of his sons. He had two interviews with Lincoln in the White House. Until his death, Douglass continued to fight the discrimination and segregation that Emancipation had not ended.

WALT WHITMAN
(1819–1892)

Long accepted as a major poet, not only of American but of world literature, Walt Whitman celebrated himself while at the same time praising both the average man and the uniqueness of the individual. Born on Long Island and raised in poverty in Brooklyn, Whitman went to school for only five or six years. He worked as a printer, schoolteacher, and editor, writing poems and stories for popular magazines. In 1855 he published at his own expense a thin book of poems called *Leaves of Grass*. The poems were unconventional, without rhyme or meter, realistic in imagery, and so intensely personal in tone they shocked some readers. During the Civil War, he volunteered his services in the capital's military hospitals, while also working as a clerk in the Department of the Interior. He had glimpsed Lincoln now and then as the President rode through the streets, and upon Lincoln's assassination, Whitman wrote the great Lincoln elegy, "When Lilacs Last in the Dooryard Bloom'd." One of his finest poems, it voices his grief over the death of Lincoln.

ULYSSES S. GRANT
(1822–1885)

Ulysses S. Grant was born in Ohio, graduated from West Point in 1843, and served in the Mexican War, which he called the most disgraceful war the country had ever fought. He hated the routine of army life, took to drinking, and resigned from the army in 1854. Then, in 1861, he entered the Union army with the rank of brigadier-general. In Ulysses S. Grant, Lincoln finally found a general who could win battles and end the war. Grant rose rapidly as he won first small victories and then major campaigns, climaxing in Lee's surrender and the downfall of the Confederacy. Having earned great fame, Grant became the Republican choice for President and was elected in 1868 and 1872. But he was a poor judge of men and politics and his administration was tainted by corruption. After leaving office, he was swindled out of his money by a Wall Street operator. His old friend Mark Twain offered to publish his *Personal Memoirs* to save him from bankruptcy. Grant completed it in 1885, while dying of cancer, and the memoirs brought the family nearly $500,000—the largest royalties ever paid an author up to that time.

Lincoln and the World
Around Him: A Chronology

IF LINCOLN HAD BEEN A MAJOR ARTIST OR ATHLETE OR EXPLORER, THERE would have been numerous achievements to list in a chronology of his life. But Lincoln's life was nothing like that. The great achievement the world recognizes him for is his conduct of the Civil War, the most wrenching experience the nation has yet endured. And this capstone of his otherwise quiet and obscure life consumed but his last four years on earth. In those four years he did not lead armies in the field to chalk up great victories like some Napoleon. No, but his was the great mind and the noble spirit that made possible the preservation of the Union and the abolition of slavery.

That mind and that spirit are best recorded in the words Lincoln spoke or wrote. This timeline will help the reader trace the events of his life and to glimpse the larger background of his time.

1809   **Abraham Lincoln born February 12 in Kentucky, of pioneer farmer and carpenter Thomas Lincoln and Nancy Hanks Lincoln.** James Madison inaugurated fourth U.S. president.

1810   U.S. Census shows population of 7.2 million, including 60,000 immigrants and about 1.2 million slaves.

1811   First steamboat sails down the Mississippi River to New Orleans.

1812   War declared against Great Britain. *Grimm's Fairy Tales* published. Madison reelected president.

1813   Jane Austen publishes *Pride and Prejudice*.

1814   Creek War ends with Indian removal.

1815   **Lincoln begins attending school for short periods.** General Andrew Jackson defeats British at Battle of New Orleans after peace treaty is signed. Napoleon's army defeated at Waterloo.

1816   **Lincoln family moves to Indiana.** James Monroe elected president.

1817   Construction of the Erie Canal begins.

1818   **Lincoln's mother dies.**

1819   **Lincoln's father marries Sarah Bush Johnston, widow.**

1820   South becomes world's largest cotton producer. Congress passes Missouri Compromise, banning slavery north of latitude 36° 30′. Monroe reelected president. John Keats publishes poems.

1821   Mexico wins independence from Spain. First public high school in United States opens, in Boston. First women's college opens, in Troy, New York. Indian removal to West begins.

1822   Denmark Vesey's slave rebellion suppressed. Cotton mills begin production in Massachusetts with water-powered machinery.

1823   Monroe Doctrine proclaimed. James Fenimore Cooper publishes first Leatherstocking tale. William Wilberforce forms antislavery society in England.

1824 **Lincoln attends school in fall and winter; helps with plowing and planting; works for hire; begins reading widely.** Beethoven composes Ninth Symphony.

1825 John Quincy Adams chosen president by House of Representatives.

1826 First short-line railroads built.

1827 **Lincoln works as boatman and farmhand.** *Freedom's Journal,* first African-American newspaper, appears.

1828 **Lincoln on flatboat trip to New Orleans with farm produce cargo; returns home by steamboat; develops interest in law after observing county courthouse trials.** Democratic Party forms and elects Andrew Jackson president. Nathaniel Hawthorne publishes first novel, *Fanshawe.*

1829 Workingmen's Party formed in New York.

1830 **Lincoln's family moves to Illinois; he makes first political speech.** Mexico abolishes slavery in Texas. Religious revival movement begins. Mormon Church founded.

1831 **Lincoln makes second flatboat trip, taking cargo to New Orleans; leaves family and moves alone to New Salem, Illinois, where he works in a general store, does odd jobs, and joins the local debating club.** Nat Turner's slave revolt in Virginia. William Lloyd Garrison begins publishing *The Liberator.* John Greenleaf Whittier and Edgar Allan Poe publish poems.

1832 Lincoln loses election to Illinois legislature; volunteers for militia in Black Hawk War; becomes partner in New Salem general store. Jackson reelected president. Samuel F. B. Morse invents the telegraph.

1833 Lincoln's store fails; deeply in debt, he boards with various families and works as a hired hand. He becomes New Salem's postmaster, studies surveying, and is appointed deputy surveyor of Sangamon County. American Anti-Slavery Society founded. Lydia Maria Child publishes first study of racism.

1834 Lincoln is elected by new Whig Party to Illinois House of Representatives; begins study of law. Cyrus McCormick patents reaper. Anti-abolitionist riots in New York and Philadelphia. Slavery abolished in the British Empire.

1835 Lincoln serves on many special legislative committees, helps draft bills and resolutions, supports public financing of internal improvements. Charles Dickens publishes first book.

1836 Lincoln wins reelection to legislature; receives license to practice law. Martin Van Buren elected president. Ralph Waldo Emerson publishes *Nature*. Massachusetts adopts child labor law.

1837 Lincoln protests legislature's resolutions against abolitionists. When state moves capital from Vandalia to Springfield, Lincoln moves to the new capital, where he begins a civil and criminal law practice. Financial panic triggers seven-year depression. Nathaniel Hawthorne publishes *Twice-Told Tales*. John Deere invents first plow with steel moldboard.

1838   **Lincoln reelected to legislature; nominated for speaker by Whigs but defeated by a Democrat; serves as Whig floor leader.** Cherokee Indians on "Trail of Tears" to West. Morse Code introduced.

1839   **Lincoln begins extensive trips on judicial circuit; meets Mary Todd of prominent Kentucky family.** John James Audubon publishes *Birds of America*. Photography invented by Louis Daguerre, French physicist. First teacher-training school started, in Massachusetts.

1840   **Lincoln campaigns for Whig presidential candidate, William Henry Harrison, who wins election. Lincoln reelected to legislature; engaged to Mary Todd in the fall.** Immigration to United States rises. Federal workers gain ten-hour day. World Anti-Slavery Convention meets in London. Liberty Party formed on antislavery platform. Utopian communities founded. Edgar Allan Poe publishes short stories.

1841   **Lincoln breaks engagement with Mary Todd; forms new law partnership; wins appeal before Illinois Supreme Court. On steamboat trip home from Kentucky he sees chained slaves.** Harrison dies; John Tyler is first vice president to succeed to presidency. John C. Frémont explores route to Oregon. Henry W. Longfellow publishes *Ballads and Other Poems*.

1842   **Lincoln decides against another race for legislature; renews courtship of Mary Todd and marries her on November 4, and they move into room in tavern.** Seminoles forced to move west.

1843   Lincoln tries for but fails to get Whig nomination for Congress; first child, Robert Todd Lincoln, born August 1, and the family moves into a rented cottage.

1844   Lincoln buys house in Springfield—family home until 1861; dissolves law partnership and takes on young William Herndon as new partner; campaigns for Whig leader, Henry Clay, but Democrat James K. Polk wins presidential election. Republic of Texas annexed to United States. First private bath in American hotel installed in New York. YMCA founded in England.

1845   Lincoln's law practice flourishes; earns about $1,500 a year. Ex-slave Frederick Douglass publishes autobiography. Term "Manifest Destiny" coined. Blight of Ireland's potato crop causes Great Famine and mass migration to America.

1846   Lincolns have second son, Edward Baker Lincoln, born March 10. Lincoln is elected to U.S. House of Representatives. United States declares war against Mexico. Wilmot Proviso introduced in Congress to limit extension of slavery. Michigan first state to abolish capital punishment. Fyodor Dostoyevski publishes *Poor Folk*, first Russian social novel. Elias Howe patents sewing machine. First recorded baseball game, played in Hoboken, NJ.

1847   Lincoln takes seat in Congress and moves family to a boardinghouse near the Capitol; presents "spot" resolutions in House. Mormon migration to Utah begins. Frederick Douglass launches abolitionist paper. Brontë sisters publish their first novels—Charlotte's *Jane Eyre* and Emily's *Wuthering Heights*.

1848   Lincoln serves on three congressional committees; attacks Polk's war policy in speech and votes to ban slavery in any territory acquired from Mexico. Lincoln does not run for second term in Congress but campaigns in several states for Whig candidate, General Zachary Taylor, who is elected president. Free Soil Party formed, opposing slavery in new U.S. territories. Treaty of Guadalupe Hidalgo ends war with Mexico. First women's rights convention held in Seneca Falls, New York. Karl Marx and Friedrich Engels publish *Communist Manifesto*.

1849   At end of his term in Congress, Lincoln votes to ban slavery in federal territories and to abolish the slave trade in the District of Columbia; resumes law practice in Illinois. First railroad west of Mississippi is chartered. Elizabeth Blackwell is first woman in the world to receive a medical degree.

1850   Lincoln's son Edward dies on February 1; third son, William Wallace (Willie), born December 21. Lincoln returns to spring and fall rounds of judicial circuit. U.S. Census shows population of 23 million, including about 3.2 million slaves and about 1.7 million immigrants. Congress agrees on Compromise of 1850, including stronger Fugitive Slave Act and abolition of slave trade in District of Columbia. President Taylor dies and Vice President Millard Fillmore becomes president. First national convention of women advocating vote for women is held in Worcester, Massachusetts. Hawthorne publishes *The Scarlet Letter*.

1851   Lincoln's father dies on January 17. Herman Melville publishes *Moby-Dick*.

1852   Lincoln campaigns for Whig presidential candidate, Winfield Scott, who loses to Democrat Franklin Pierce. Harriet Beecher Stowe publishes *Uncle Tom's Cabin*. Massachusetts adopts nation's first effective school attendance law.

1853   Lincoln's fourth son, Thomas (Tad), born April 4. Children's Aid Society established in New York. U.S. makes Gadsden Purchase from Mexico, acquiring what is now southern New Mexico and Arizona. Antioch College, welcoming male and female students, opens in Ohio.

1854   **Lincoln speaks against Kansas-Nebraska Act, repealing antislavery provisions of Missouri Compromise. He is elected to Illinois legislature but declines seat in order to become eligible for election to U.S. Senate.** Republican Party is formed in reaction against Kansas-Nebraska Act. Henry David Thoreau publishes *Walden*. Large-scale immigration from China begins, supplying manpower to build transcontinental railroad.

1855   **Lincoln fails to be elected to U.S. Senate by Illinois legislature. His legal practice for railroads raises his annual income to about $5,000.** Massachusetts bans segregated public schools. Walt Whitman publishes *Leaves of Grass*. Settlement of Kansas under "popular sovereignty" doctrine leads to bloody struggle between pro- and antislavery forces.

1856   **Lincoln helps found Republican Party in Illinois and campaigns for its presidential candidate, John C. Frémont;** the Democrat James Buchanan is elected. Trolley cars pulled by steam engines begin operating in New England. Gail Borden gets patent for condensing milk.

1857   **Lincoln gives major speech against Dred Scott Decision of U.S. Supreme Court.** Panic of 1857. Frederick Law Olmsted and Calvert Vaux design Central Park in New York. Gustave Flaubert publishes *Madame Bovary*. Louis Pasteur proves fermentation is caused by microbes.

1858   Lincoln accepts Republican nomination for U.S. Senate and debates his opponent Stephen Douglas on slavery issue seven times while making many other speeches throughout Illinois. Republicans win plurality in election but not control of legislature. Kansas voters make their territory nonslaveholding. First successful transatlantic telegraph cable laid. Stagecoach service begins between San Francisco and St. Louis.

1859   Lincoln loses to Douglas when Illinois legislature chooses Douglas for senator. For several months Lincoln campaigns for Republican candidates in Midwest and hears his name mentioned as a possible presidential nominee. John Brown raids Harpers Ferry and is hanged. First successful oil well drilled, in Pennsylvania. Work begins on Suez Canal. Charles Darwin publishes *Origin of Species*.

1860   Lincoln delivers address on slavery at Cooper Union in New York and makes speaking tour of New England. At Republican Convention in Chicago he wins nomination for president on the third ballot; following custom he does not make campaign speeches. He wins the presidency in a four-party contest. South Carolina secedes from Union on December 20 and several other Southern states follow in the next few months.

1861   Lincoln selects Cabinet and is inaugurated on March 4. The Civil War begins when Confederates fire on Fort Sumter on April 12. Confederate States of America formed. Lincoln summons troops and expands army and navy, appointing George McClellan commander of the army. Lincoln recommends emancipation and colonization for slaves confiscated from Confederate owners; first Battle of Bull Run; Lincoln blockades South. First federal income tax enacted. Mathew Brady begins photographing the Civil War.

1862 Lincoln takes direct command of Union armies and signs law abolishing slavery in the District of Columbia. He approves law banning slavery in the territories, and he issues preliminary Emancipation Proclamation on September 22, to take effect on January 1, 1863. Lincoln establishes the Department of Agriculture and signs the Homestead Act and bill providing land grants for agricultural colleges. Lincoln's son Willie dies on February 20. Battles of Shiloh, Bull Run, and Antietam.

1863 Lincoln issues Emancipation Proclamation on January 1, freeing all slaves in Confederate-held territory; signs laws introducing military conscription and creating national banking system; delivers Gettysburg Address on November 19; offers amnesty to all Southerners taking loyalty oath to Union. Draft riots in northern cities.

1864 Lincoln appoints Ulysses S. Grant general-in-chief of Union armies; William T. Sherman marches through Georgia. Lincoln is reelected, defeating the Democrat George McClellan. Cheyenne and Arapaho massacred at Sand Creek, Colorado. Pasteur develops method of pasteurization used in milk. George Pullman creates sleeping car.

1865 Lincoln wins congressional support for Thirteenth Amendment abolishing slavery; signs bill to create federal relief bureau of freedpeople and refugees; gives Second Inaugural Address on March 4. Lee surrenders to Grant on April 9. On April 11 Lincoln makes last speech, dealing with problems of Reconstruction of the South. Lincoln is shot by John Wilkes Booth at Ford's Theater in Washington on the night of April 14 and dies at 7:22 A.M. on April 15. Andrew Johnson becomes president.

A Note on Sources

THE WORDS OF LINCOLN CONTAINED IN THIS BOOK MAY BE FOUND IN COM-
plete form in various scholarly editions. The first major collection of Lincoln's writings, *The Complete Works of Abraham Lincoln,* was edited by
John G. Nicolay and John Hay, who had served as his secretaries in the
White House. Two volumes were published in 1894 and expanded into
twelve volumes in 1905.

Later, another edition of Lincoln's words appeared, correcting errors
or changes made in the Nicolay–Hay edition, adding material discovered
after its publication. This was *The Collected Works of Abraham Lincoln,*
edited by Roy P. Basler, assisted by Marion Dolores Pratt and Lloyd A.
Dunlap. This edition appeared in nine volumes from 1953 to 1955. As
additional material was gathered, it was published in supplements in 1974
and 1990, edited by Roy P. Basler and Christian O. Basler.

In 1989, the Library of America published *Lincoln* in two volumes,
which includes the texts of 795 letters, speeches, messages, proclamations,
orders, memoranda, drafts, and fragments written or delivered by Lincoln
between 1832 and 1865. These were selected and annotated by the historian Don E. Fehrenbacher.

In 1990, HarperCollins published *Lincoln on Democracy,* a one-
volume selection of 140 of Lincoln's writings edited by Harold Holzer with
a preface by Mario M. Cuomo, and including essays by seven Lincoln

scholars. In 1992, Viking Penguin published *The Portable Abraham Lincoln*, edited by Andrew Delbanco. The selected texts were printed without deletions.

My own edition, prepared especially for younger readers, owes much to the scholarship of those who edited the earlier collections.

Readers who wish to know more about Lincoln's life, personality, and actions will find vast stores of information and opinion in the libraries. More books about him appear annually, for writers find him to be one of the most fascinating figures in our past. The most recent biography is Stephen B. Oates's *With Malice Toward None: The Life of Abraham Lincoln*, Harper & Row, 1977. Earlier, Carl Sandburg wrote a two-volume life, *Abraham Lincoln: The Prairie Years* and *Abraham Lincoln: The War Years*, Harcourt Brace Jovanovich, 1939. It is an uncritical biography, but movingly conveys a poet's sympathy for a great and beloved man.

Pictorial biographies of Lincoln include Stefan Lorant's *The Life of Abraham Lincoln*, Signet, 1954, and Russell Freedman's *Lincoln: A Photobiography*, Clarion, 1987.

Many studies have been published on Lincoln's attitute toward slavery and equal rights, his relations with African-Americans, and his policies affecting them. Among these are *Lincoln and Black Freedom: A Study in Presidential Leadership* by LaWanda Cox, University of Illinois, 1985, and Benjamin Quarles's *Lincoln and the Negro*, Russell & Russell, 1968. John Hope Franklin's *The Emancipation Proclamation*, Doubleday, 1963, is a fine history of the development of that document and its impact.

What scholars consider to be the best contribution to the many studies of the Gettysburg Address is *Lincoln at Gettysburg: The Words That Remade America* by Gary Wills, Simon & Schuster, 1992. Wills says the great achievement of the "prose-poem" was to bring America a giant step closer to the ideal affirmed by the Declaration of Independence and to explain why in fascinating detail.

Lincoln day to day during his presidency is captured in intimate detail by Margaret Leech in *Reveille in Washington*, Harper, 1941, and by Noah Brooks, a wartime reporter and friend of Lincoln, in his *Washington in Lincoln's Time*, edited by P.J. Staudemaus, T. Yoselof, 1967.

Perhaps the best one-volume treatment of the Civil War is James M. McPherson's *Battle Cry of Freedom: The Civil War Era*, Oxford University Press, 1988. For the story of the struggle in the White House, in Congress, and in the country to shape the postwar era, see Eric Foner's *Reconstruction: America's Unfinished Revolution 1863–1877*, Harper & Row, 1988.

Three eminent historians have given us collections of their superb essays on Lincoln and his time. One is James M. McPherson, *Abraham Lincoln and the Second American Revolution*, Oxford University Press, 1990. Another is Don E. Fehrenbacher, *Lincoln in Text and Context*, Stanford University Press, 1987. The third is Stephen B. Oates, *Abraham Lincoln: The Man Behind the Myths*, Harper & Row, 1984.

For those who wish to pursue special aspects of Lincoln's life and work, the bibliography is immense. There are books about his philosophy, the press's treatment of him, his literary style, his politics, leadership, religion, youth, marriage and family, his medical condition, his view of civil liberties, his myth or image, his speeches, the Lincoln–Douglas debates, and books by or about his generals, his friends, his cabinet members, and his political opponents. And of course, there are innumerable studies of the battles of the Civil War.

Illustrator's Note

DESCRIPTIONS OF THE HORRORS OF SLAVERY, THE TERRIBLE CONFLICTS OF the Civil War, the drama that was Lincoln's life, and the soulful expression captured miraculously in several photographic portraits of Lincoln made an indelible impression upon me at a very early age, and since then have continued to stir my imagination. I saw this book as a rare opportunity to give expression and tangible shape to the multitude of haunting and symbolic images that the name Abraham Lincoln has conjured up in my mind for as long as I can remember. For this reason, the images that I have created do not aspire to be literal translations of any particular passages found in the text. Instead, wishing to see Lincoln through the impressionable eyes of a child, I strove to create symbols that could best express and pay homage to the larger-than-life quality that Lincoln's life and legend possess.

Readers will note that the book opens with a bold portrait of Lincoln depicted as a vibrant sun that both dominates and nourishes the farmland below. In the end, however, Lincoln undergoes a transformation—the book closes with a melancholy portrait of Lincoln in the guise of a crescent moon, tipped slightly downward. I hope the analogy I have drawn between Lincoln and the proverbial man in the moon will express the way I have always felt about Lincoln and his legacy: like the man in the moon above us, Lincoln is universal, timeless, and omnipresent. Looming large above us in our collective imaginations, Lincoln's specter haunts us with his destiny and our own, reminding us of our limitations but also of our potential to overcome such limitations. In many ways he has become our conscience, a meter by which we measure right and wrong.

Above all, the memory of Abraham Lincoln is, like the man in the moon, a comforting and reassuring presence, casting a beam of light our way—a light we can always turn to for inspiration but that we must never take for granted.

"Black is noble," proclaimed the great French artist Odilon Redon almost a century ago. With that inspired conviction so simply stated fresh in my mind, I momentarily cast aside the complex color printmaking techniques I had been employing and returned to the directness and simplicity of the black-and-white linocut. I then commenced to work on the series of prints that adorn this collection of Lincoln's writings.

The challenge that inevitably faces the artist who chooses to make linoleum cuts lies in bringing the surface of this unique and versatile material to life. Since the linoleum block possesses no texture or grain of its own, whatever tonal gradations, ornamentations, or patterns that appear in the final print must be deliberately invented. It is a medium that requires the utmost economy of means by the artist, forcing one to distill one's images and successfully translate them into graphic textures, signs, and patterns that can effectively be cut. A print is in fact a "mirror" image of the original drawing on the block. Consequently, the artist works in reverse, not only in the sense of one's orientation of left and right but in terms of the positive and negative elements as well, requiring considerable foresight on the part of the artist. Furthermore, what one cuts away cannot be put back, making this a most unforgiving medium. It is precisely the vigor, boldness, and uncompromising discipline demanded of the artist that makes this medium such a healthy and challenging one.

The images reproduced in this book are greatly reduced from the originals. The vertical portraits of Lincoln's contemporaries all measure 15″ wide × 19½″ tall. The various portraits of Lincoln are either 10″ × 13″, 13″ × 17″, or 15″ × 19½″. The horizontal spreads are either 21½″ × 13″ or 24½″ × 15″. All of the decorative chapter opener borders are 10″ × 13″. The decorative round cuts measure 6″ in diameter.

The image reproduced on the cover of this book is a "reduction print." Invented by Pablo Picasso (1881–1973) in 1959, a reduction print is a polychrome linocut made with the use of a single block. Through a series of progressive cuttings, inkings, and printings, the image slowly emerges while, paradoxically, the actual block is destroyed. A reduction print can therefore never be reprinted. This print, measuring 28″ × 17″, belongs to a limited edition of eighteen signed and numbered prints.

—Stephen Alcorn

Index

Numbers in italics refer to the illustrated portraits.